LEARNING AND REASONING IN HYBRID STRUCTURED SPACES

Frontiers in Artificial Intelligence and Applications

The book series Frontiers in Artificial Intelligence and Applications (FAIA) covers all aspects of theoretical and applied Artificial Intelligence research in the form of monographs, selected doctoral dissertations, handbooks and proceedings volumes. The FAIA series contains several sub-series, including 'Information Modelling and Knowledge Bases' and 'Knowledge-Based Intelligent Engineering Systems'. It also includes the biennial European Conference on Artificial Intelligence (ECAI) proceedings volumes, and other EurAI (European Association for Artificial Intelligence, formerly ECCAI) sponsored publications. The series has become a highly visible platform for the publication and dissemination of original research in this field. Volumes are selected for inclusion by an international editorial board of well-known scholars in the field of AI. All contributions to the volumes in the series have been peer reviewed.

The FAIA series is indexed in ACM Digital Library; DBLP; EI Compendex; Google Scholar; Scopus; Web of Science: Conference Proceedings Citation Index – Science (CPCI-S) and Book Citation Index – Science (BKCI-S); Zentralblatt MATH.

Volume 350

Recently published in this series

ISSN 0922-6389 (print)
ISSN 1879-8314 (online)

Learning and Reasoning in Hybrid Structured Spaces

Paolo Morettin

Department of Computer Science, KU Leuven, Belgium

IOS Press

Amsterdam • Berlin • Washington, DC

ISBN 978-1-64368-266-2 (print)
ISBN 978-1-64368-267-9 (online)
Library of Congress Control Number: 2022934987
doi: 10.3233/FAIA350

PhD Dissertation, approved by the University of Trento, Italy
Date of the defense: May 2020
Advisor: Andrea Passerini, University of Trento
Co-Advisor: Roberto Sebastiani, University of Trento

Publisher
IOS Press BV
Nieuwe Hemweg 6B
1013 BG Amsterdam
Netherlands
fax: +31 20 687 0019
e-mail: order@iospress.nl

For book sales in the USA and Canada:
IOS Press, Inc.
6751 Tepper Drive
Clifton, VA 20124
USA
Tel.: +1 703 830 6300
Fax: +1 703 830 2300
sales@iospress.com

LEGAL NOTICE
The publisher is not responsible for the use which might be made of the following information.

Abstract

Many real world AI applications involve reasoning on both continuous and discrete variables, while requiring some level of symbolic reasoning that can provide guarantees on the system's behaviour. Unfortunately, most of the existing probabilistic models do not efficiently support hard constraints or they are limited to purely discrete or continuous scenarios. Weighted Model Integration (WMI) is a recent and general formalism that enables probabilistic modeling and inference in hybrid structured domains. A difference of WMI-based inference algorithms with respect to most alternatives is that probabilities are computed inside a structured support involving both logical and algebraic relationships between variables. While some progress has been made in the last years and the topic is increasingly gaining interest from the community, research in this area is at an early stage. These aspects motivate the study of hybrid and symbolic probabilistic models and the development of scalable inference procedures and effective learning algorithms in these domains. This PhD Thesis embodies my effort in studying scalable reasoning and learning techniques in the context of WMI.

Acknowledgments

Now that's almost over, I can say it has been a fun ride. This crazy-fast, colorful journey wouldn't have been the same without the wonderful people I met along the way. Thank you Andrea, thank you Roberto for your kindness and patience in guiding me through these challenging years. Doing a PhD under your supervision has been a life-changing experience and one of the best decisions I've ever made. Life in Trento wouldn't have been as joyful without Marco, Stefano, Dragone, Gianni, Luca, Gianluca and the whole SML family, Edoardo, Zaki, Alessandra, Daniele, Sivam, Genc, Mesay.. I couldn't hope for more supportive and easy-going pals to hang with. I would like to thank Luc, Samuel, Guy, Antonio, Zhe, Fanqi and all the people I met during my visits at KU Leuven and UCLA. Thank you for being so welcoming, working with you was a pleasure and a privilege. Un grazie a Maurizio, Efrem, Matteo, Dozzi, Fabio, Alessandro, Giulia, Lucia, Jacopo, Ceci, Damiano, Fabi, Usha, Giovi, Pola. Tutti questi anni assieme mi hanno insegnato cosa voglia dire amicizia. Non avrei mai potuto arrivare in fondo a questo percorso senza il supporto della mia famiglia. Grazie a Ilario, Liliana e Daniele per essere una fonte inesauribile di affetto, ispirazione e coraggio. Grazie Alessia per aver portato gioia e amore nella mia vita.

Thank you Pollo, so long.

Contents

CHAPTER 1

INTRODUCTION

1.1 Motivation

Artificial intelligence applications often times involve dealing with uncertainty, such as a partially observed environment or noisy observations. Probability theory is a principled way of modelling uncertainty. Thanks to their sound theoretical foundations, their data efficiency and interpretability, probabilistic models find applications in many fields, such as bioinformatics [42], finance [67] and robotics [99]. Many complex real world applications involve reasoning on both continuous and discrete variables. Unfortunately, most of the current probabilistic models are incapable of dealing with hybrid numerical and logical domains. Existing hybrid continuous/discrete models are typically limited in expressiveness by distributional assumptions or support approximate inference only, with no guarantees on the approximation error. This implies that many real world problems are out of reach of the current systems, making the development of more expressive models a relevant research direction.

Although most of the recent research focuses on end-to-end sub-symbolic models, many real world applications require some level of symbolic reasoning that can provide guarantees on the system's behaviour. This aspect is pivotal in safety-critical applications and policy-making [89]. At the same time, it has been shown that providing structured prior knowledge on the domain is beneficial in many learning tasks, in particular when the availability of training data is limited [106], or unlabelled for a specific task [100]. Unfortunately, there is limited literature on learning hybrid structured probabilistic models. Enabling scalable probabilistic inference in these domains is thus an important research direction also from a learning perspective.

Weighted Model Integration (WMI) [10] is a recent and general formalism that enables probabilistic modeling and inference in hybrid structured domains. WMI is a generalized form of Weighted Model Counting (WMC), a state-of-the-art technique for probabilistic inference in the purely discrete case. A key difference of WMI with respect to most inference algorithms is that probabilities are computed in the constrained space that is explicitly defined by a structured support. The support of the distribution can be a complex formula involving both logical and algebraic relationships between variables. While some progress has been made in the last years and the topic is increasingly gaining interest from the community, research in this area is at an early stage. Much work has to be done in tracing the complexity boundaries of the inference problem, identifying tractable subclasses of problems and studying the many issues related with learning WMI distributions from data. In particular, structure learning is an unexplored research direction.

Probabilistic inference is notoriously a computationally hard problem, even in simpler domains. Thus, hybrid probabilistic inference in structured spaces is a particularly challenging task. Nonetheless, advancements in this area have a potential to bring benefits in many high-impact applications. These aspects motivate the study of hybrid and symbolic probabilistic models and the development of scalable inference procedures and effective learning algorithms in these domains.

1.2   Contributions

This PhD thesis embodies my effort in studying scalable reasoning and learning techniques in the context of WMI. My research on this topic focused on the following aspects:

- improving over the state-of-the-art algorithms for exact probabilistic inference;

- studying tractability of WMI problems;

- investigating the problem of learning the structure and parameters of WMI distributions from data.

The content of this manuscript is mainly based upon the following articles:

[78] "Efficient Weighted Model Integration via SMT-Based Predicate Abstraction". Morettin, P.; Passerini, A.; Sebastiani, R. In *International Joint Conference on Artificial Intelligence (IJCAI)*, 2017.

[77] "Advanced SMT techniques for weighted model integration". Morettin, P.; Passerini, A.; Sebastiani, R. In *Journal of Artificial Intelligence (AIJ)*, 2019.

[110] "Hybrid Probabilistic Inference with Logical Constraints: Tractability and Message-Passing". Zeng, Z.; Yan, F.; Morettin, P.; Vergari, A.; Van den Broeck, G. In *Knowledge Representation & Reasoning Meets Machine Learning (KR2ML) workshop at NeurIPS*, 2019.

[76] "Learning Weighted Model Integration Distributions". Morettin, P.; Kolb, S.; Teso, S.; Passerini, A. In *Proceedings of AAAI*, 2020.

While the content of this thesis focuses on theory, I also contributed to *pywmi* [51][1], a Python3 library that unifies the technical efforts of different research groups into a single framework for WMI modelling and inference.

---

[1]`https://github.com/weighted-model-integration/pywmi`

1.3 Outline of the Thesis

The rest of the manuscript is structured as follows:

Chapter 2: Background A brief introduction on the theoretic concepts this thesis builds on. Specifically, this chapter covers Probabilistic Graphical Models and inference algorithms based on reducing the problem to Weighted Model Counting/Integration.

Chapter 3: Related work This chapter summarizes the related work in hybrid probabilistic models with a focus on alternative techniques for WMI and similar formalisms, hybrid density estimation and learning of structured distributions subject to hard constraints.

Chapter 4: WMI-PA This chapter presents WMI-PA, an exact, solver-based WMI algorithm that leverages SMT-based *predicate abstraction* techniques for exploiting the structural properties of the weight function, thus reducing the number of integrations required to compute the weighted model integral. This algorithm is based on a revised formulation of the problem, introduced in section 4.2. Section 4.3 describes a real-world case study that motivates the performance gain obtained by reasoning on the conditions that govern the behaviour of the unnormalized density. The formal description of WMI-PA and an empirical evaluation of its performance are reported in sections 4.4 and 4.5.

Chapter 5: MP-MI A different approach to the WMI problem is presented in this chapter. Section 5.1 reports a theoretical result that describes how WMI problems can be reduced to a MI problem under some conditions. Tractability boundaries for the unweighted case are formally investigated in section 5.2. Then, section 5.3 presents an exact message-passing algorithm, dubbed MP-MI, that enables efficient probabilistic inference and moments computation in some families of distributions. Finally, the performance of MP-MI on these families of MI problems is studied in section 5.4.

Chapter 6: LARIAT In section 6.1, we first introduce the problem of learning a WMI distribution, then we present LARIAT, the first approach to this problem. The method separately learns the structured support and estimates the density inside the feasible hybrid space, ultimately renormalizing the density to account for the learned constraints. Section 6.2 provides an empirical evaluation of the method on both synthetic and real world settings.

Chapter 7: Conclusion This chapter summarizes the presented work and concludes the thesis with an overview of the future work related to the topics presented here.

CHAPTER 2

BACKGROUND

In this chapter, we briefly touch upon the core concepts of probabilistic reasoning over hybrid and constrained spaces. Specifically, we will first introduce inference techniques on traditional probabilistic graphical models, then we will introduce weighted model counting as a technique for computing marginal inference over a structured space. After that, we will generalize these ideas to hybrid continuous/discrete domain by discussing the language of satisfiability modulo theories and marginalization via weighted model integration.

2.1 Probabilistic Graphical Models

Probabilistic Graphical Models [53, 45] (PGMs) are well known approaches for modelling uncertainty and implement systems that are capable of making informed decisions in a partially observed environment. *Probability theory* is the formal framework that allows PGMs to deal with uncertainty in a principled manner. In these models, the *observed* and the *latent* stochastic variables are represented as nodes in a graph, while the edges encode some probabilistic (in)dependencies. The resulting graph, often called the *structure* of the probabilistic model, is augmented with functions that weight local configurations according to their probabilities. Using these two ingredients, PGMs encode a *joint probability distribution* over its variables in a compact, factorized form. Explicitly encoding certain independencies in the graphical structure has two main benefits:

- it allows representing a highly dimensional distribution compactly, while an unstructured table would have size exponential in the number of variables. Moreover, the regularities and (conditional) independencies in the structure can be leveraged by the inference procedures;

- the resulting probabilistic graphical model is usually much more interpretable compared to alternative approaches, thus allowing human experts to better understand the model and its decisions.

These aspects contributed to the adoption of PGMs in a wide range of applications, such as biological and medical informatics [42] and robotics [99]. Most PGMs are trained in a generative fashion to model the full joint distribution, thus supporting a larger number of probabilistic queries with respect to discriminative models. PGMs are usually divided into *directed* and *undirected* graphical models, called Bayesian Networks and Markov Networks respectively. These two formalism are not equivalent, as they can encode different families of joint probability distributions.

What follows is a brief introduction on PGMs, for additional reference the reader can consult [11, 53].

2.1.1 Bayesian Networks

Bayesian Networks (BNs) model the conditional dependencies between variables with a directed acyclic graph $\mathcal{G}$ and factorize the joint probability parameterized by Θ as the product of conditional probabilities between each variables with respect to its parents, or marginals for the variables having no parents. BNs are usually adopted for capturing the causal relationships between the variables, such as those occurring between the symptoms and a potential disease. More formally, a BN $\mathcal{B} \stackrel{\text{def}}{=} \langle \mathcal{G}, \Theta \rangle$ encodes the joint probability distribution over variables $\mathbf{X} = \{X_1, ..., X_N\}$:

$$P(\mathbf{X}|\Theta) \stackrel{\text{def}}{=} \prod_{i=1}^{N} P(X_i|Pa_{\mathcal{G}}(X_i), \Theta_i)$$

where $Pa_{\mathcal{G}}(X_i)$ denotes the set of parents of X_i in $\mathcal{G}$ and Θ_i is the subset of parameters that govern the probability of X_i. The independence assumptions encoded in BNs enable a more compact representation of the joint probability over the variables. Usually, the parameters of the BN are represented with *conditional probability tables* (CPTs). Modelling a joint categorical distribution over N K-ary variables $X_1, ..., X_N$ with a BN requires

$$|\Theta| = \sum_{i=1}^{N} (K-1) \cdot K^{Pa_{\mathcal{G}}(X_i)}$$

parameters instead of K^N.

Example 1. The BN $\mathcal{B} \stackrel{\text{def}}{=} \langle \mathcal{G}, \Theta \rangle$, with $\mathcal{G}$ depicted in figure 2.1, models the following joint distribution over the binary variables An (Andrea goes to the conference), Pa (Paolo goes to the conference) and Po (Pollo goes to the conference):

$$P(An, Pa, Po) = P(Po|An, Pa) \cdot P(Pa|An) \cdot P(An)$$

The parameters Θ are encoded in the CPTs:

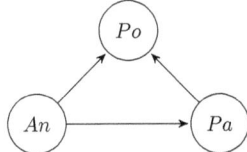

Figure 2.1: The graphical representation of the structure of the BN in Ex. 1, modelling the probabilities of Andrea, Paolo and Pollo of being at a machine learning conference.

$P(An)$
0.7

An	$P(Pa\|An)$
⊤	0.3
⊥	0.2

An	Pa	$P(Po\|An, Pa)$
⊤	⊤	1
⊤	⊥	0.4
⊥	⊤	0.6
⊥	⊥	0

With this factorization, the full joint probability can be represented using one less parameter $(2^2 + 2 + 1)$ with respect to the 2^3 parameters used by an exhaustive tabular representation.

2.1.1.1 Conditional independence

The structure of a graphical model encodes some independence assumptions between the stochastic variables. Many inference algorithms in graphical models go beyond that and try to leverage conditional independence to further decompose the problem in separate computations involving disjoint sets of variables. Fortunately, the conditional independencies can be readily inferred from $\mathcal{G}$ without requiring any analytical evaluation of the joint probability expression.

Two variables A, B are *conditionally independent* given C (denoted with $A \perp\!\!\!\perp B \mid C$) if $P(A, B|C) = P(A|C) \cdot P(B|C)$. Consider the following three structures, each one representing a different factorization of the joint probability $P(A, B, C)$ and different conditional independence assumption given C. In what follows, we consider the (undirected) path $A - C - B$ and the directionality of the edges connecting C.

C is head-to-tail

$$P(A, B, C) = P(B|C) \cdot P(C|A) \cdot P(A)$$

When none of the variables are observed, then

$$P(A, B) = P(A) \cdot \sum_C P(B|C) \cdot P(C|A)$$
$$= P(A) \cdot P(B|A)$$

Thus, it doesn't hold $A \perp\!\!\!\perp B \mid \varnothing$. On the contrary, if we condition for C, then

$$P(A, B|C) = \frac{P(A, B, C)}{P(C)}$$
$$= \frac{P(A) \cdot P(B|C)}{P(C)}$$

When C is observed, the probabilities of A and B do not interact, i.e. $A \perp\!\!\!\perp B \mid C$.

C is tail-to-tail

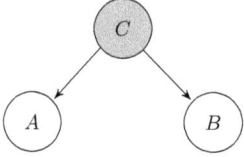

$$P(A, B, C) = P(A|C) \cdot P(B|C) \cdot P(C)$$

Again, when none of the variables are observed, $A \perp\!\!\!\perp B \mid \varnothing$, since

$$P(A, B) = \sum_C P(A|C) \cdot P(B|C) \cdot P(C)$$

doesn't factorize as $P(A) \cdot P(B)$. When conditioning for C we obtain

$$P(A, B|C) = \frac{P(A, B, C)}{P(C)} = P(A|C) \cdot P(B|C)$$

Again, this implies that $A \perp\!\!\!\perp B \mid C$.

C is head-to-head

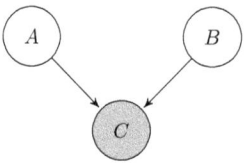

$$P(A, B, C) = P(C|A, B) \cdot P(A) \cdot P(B)$$

This third case is different from the previous ones, in fact:

$$P(A, B) = P(A) \cdot P(B) \cdot \sum_C P(C|A, B) = P(A) \cdot P(B)$$

Thus, $A \perp\!\!\!\perp B \mid \varnothing$. If we condition for C though, a dependency between the probabilities of

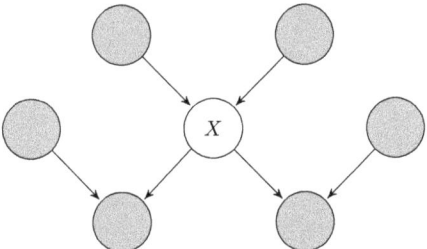

Figure 2.2: The Markov blanket of X in the directed case.

A and B is introduced.

$$P(A, B|C) = \frac{P(A) \cdot P(B) \cdot P(C|A, B)}{P(C)}$$

Thus, $A \perp\!\!\!\perp B \mid C$ doesn't hold.

The concept of *d-separation* (directed-separation) [82] generalizes the examples above to disjoint sets of variables. Given three sets of variables $\mathbf{A}$, $\mathbf{B}$, $\mathbf{C}$, the conditional independence $\mathbf{A} \perp\!\!\!\perp \mathbf{B} \mid \mathbf{C}$ can be checked by considering all the (undirected) paths in $\mathcal{G}$ between variables in $\mathbf{A}$ and $\mathbf{B}$. A path is *blocked* with respect to $\mathbf{C}$, if one of the two holds:

- the node is head-to-tail or head-to-head in the path and it is contained in $\mathbf{C}$;

- the node is tail-to-tail in the path but neither itself nor its descendants are in $\mathbf{C}$;

If every path between $\mathbf{A}$ and $\mathbf{B}$ is blocked with respect to $\mathbf{C}$, then $\mathbf{A} \perp\!\!\!\perp \mathbf{B} \mid \mathbf{C}$.

Given a variable in a BN, its *Markov blanket* is the set of its parents, its children and the children's co-parents, as depicted in figure 2.2. By the d-separation criterion, any node is independent with respect to every other node in $\mathcal{G}$ given its Markov blanket.

2.1.2 Markov Networks

Markov Networks (MNs) [47] are used to model mutual interaction between sets of variables, such as neighbouring pixels in images. A MN $\mathcal{M} \overset{\text{def}}{=} \langle \mathcal{G}, \Theta \rangle$ models undirected and possibly cyclic dependencies among variables $\mathbf{X} = \{X_1, ..., X_N\}$ using an undirected graph and factorize the joint probability as the product of non-negative *potential functions* assigned to the (maximal) cliques in the graph $Cl(\mathcal{G})$. More formally, a MN encodes the joint probability distribution

$$P(\mathbf{X}|\Theta) \overset{\text{def}}{=} \frac{1}{Z(\Theta)} \cdot \prod_{c \in Cl(\mathcal{G})} f_c(\mathbf{X}_c, \Theta_c)$$

where $\mathbf{X}_c$ denote the set of variables in the clique c, f_c is the potential associated to c, parameterized by Θ_c. Since the potentials are non-negative but not necessarily normalized, the

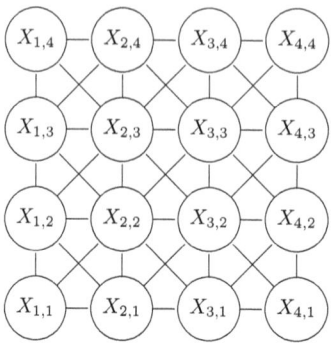

Figure 2.3: The graphical representation of the pairwise MN in Ex. 2.

partition function Z is computed as a normalizing constant

$$Z(\Theta) \stackrel{\text{def}}{=} \sum_X \prod_{c \in Cl(\mathcal{G})} f_c(\mathbf{X}_c, \Theta_c)$$

Again, assuming that the probabilistic independencies in $\mathcal{G}$ hold, a joint categorical distribution over N K-ary variables $X_1, ..., X_N$ can be modelled with

$$|\Theta| = \sum_{c \in Cl\mathcal{G}} |\mathbf{X}_c| \cdot (K-1) \cdot K^{(|\mathbf{X}_c|-1)}$$

parameters instead of $N \cdot ((K-1) \cdot K^{(N-1)})$.

Example 2. Let's consider a toy pairwise MN modelling a distribution over $N \times N$ bitmaps. The interactions between variables $\mathbf{X} = \{X_i \mid i \in [1, N]^2\}$ are modelled as pairwise relationships between neighboring pixels. The number of bivariate potential functions is equal to the number of edges of the architecture, $|\mathcal{G}_E| = 2 \cdot [(N-1)^2 + N \cdot (N-1)]$. Each potential function models the interaction of two binary variables, having $|\Theta_{i,j}| = 4$ parameters. Figure 2.3 depicts the graphical representation of a MN $\mathcal{M}$ over 4×4 bitmaps. The joint distribution modelled by $\mathcal{M}$ is

$$P(\mathbf{X}|\Theta) \stackrel{\text{def}}{=} \frac{1}{Z(\Theta)} \cdot \prod_{\{i,j\} \in \mathcal{G}_E} f_{i,j}(X_i, X_j, \Theta_{i,j})$$

Assuming that the pixels in an image are exclusively related to their neighbors is not necessarily a sound modelling assumption, but it greatly reduces the number of parameters with respect to the fully connected case with bivariate potentials, having $|\Theta| = 4 \cdot (2 + 4N^2 - 6N)$ parameters instead of $|\Theta| = 4 \cdot \frac{N^2(N^2-1)}{2}$.

2.1.3   Factor graphs

Both directed and undirected graphical models define a factorization of the joint probability. *Factor graphs* [56] represent a common formalism that captures this decomposition by explicitly introducing factor nodes. Formally, a factor graph $\mathcal{F} \stackrel{\text{def}}{=} \langle \mathcal{G}, \Theta \rangle$ is a undirected bipartite graph $\mathcal{G}$ having variable nodes $\mathbf{X}$ connected to factor nodes $\mathbf{F} = \{F_1, ..., F_K\}$. Factors nodes F_i are associated with functions of their neighbors and Θ. This unifying formalism is noteworthy as many inference algorithms can be expressed as computations on a factor graph and can thus be applied to BNs and MNs alike. A BN $\mathcal{B} \stackrel{\text{def}}{=} \langle \mathcal{G}, \Theta \rangle$ can be turned into the corresponding factor graph by first *moralizing* $\mathcal{G}$, i.e. adding an undirected edge between every parent of a node. Then, we obtain the factor graph by dropping the directionality of the edges and encoding each conditional probability $P(X_i | Pa_{\mathcal{G}}(X_i), \Theta_i)$ as a factor $f(X_i, Pa_{\mathcal{G}}(X_i), \Theta_i)$. For MNs, the conversion into factor graph is straightforward.

Example 3. Consider the BN in figure 2.4 (top), representing the joint probability distribution over $\mathbf{X} = \{X_1, X_2, X_3, X_4, X_5\}$:

$$P(\mathbf{X}|\Theta) \stackrel{\text{def}}{=} P(X_5|X_3, X_4, \Theta) \cdot P(X_4|\Theta) \cdot P(X_3|X_1, X_2, \Theta) \cdot P(X_1|\Theta) \cdot P(X_2|\Theta)$$

Using the procedure described above, we can convert it into the corresponding factor graph representation, depicted in figure 2.4 (bottom), with factors:

$$f_a(X_1, \Theta) \stackrel{\text{def}}{=} P(X_1|\Theta)$$
$$f_b(X_2, \Theta) \stackrel{\text{def}}{=} P(X_2|\Theta)$$
$$f_c(X_1, X_2, X_3, \Theta) \stackrel{\text{def}}{=} P(X_3|X_1, X_2, \Theta)$$
$$f_d(X_4, \Theta) \stackrel{\text{def}}{=} P(X_4|\Theta)$$
$$f_e(X_3, X_4, X_5, \Theta) \stackrel{\text{def}}{=} P(X_5|X_3, X_4, \Theta)$$

Being a very convenient way of representing arbitrary factorizations of joint probabilities, factor graphs are often the input representation of many inference algorithms. In the next section we will indeed introduce how to compute marginal inference over factor graphs.

2.1.4   The belief propagation algorithm

The *belief propagation algorithm* (BP) is a well known marginal inference algorithm for factor graphs [56]. The algorithm converges to the exact marginals in acyclic factor graphs. When loops are presented, variants called *loopy BP* algorithms can be used to obtain an approximate result. In the following we will cover the exact case only.

The algorithm computes for any variable node $X_i \in \mathbf{X}$ the marginal $P(X_i)$ by sending variable and factor *messages* through the edges the factor graph. A message from a variable X_i to a factor F_j is simply the product of the factor messages coming from the neighbors

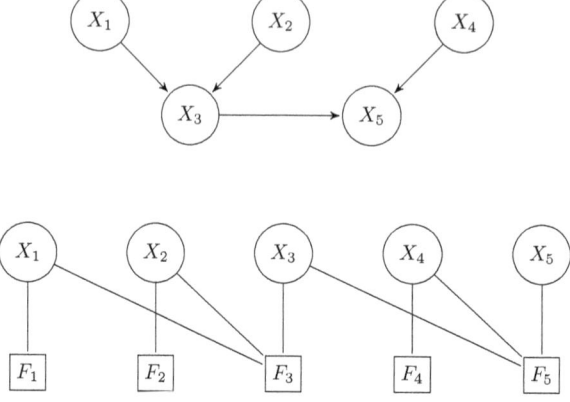

Figure 2.4: The graphical representation of the BN in Ex. 3 (top) and its factor graph counterpart (bottom).

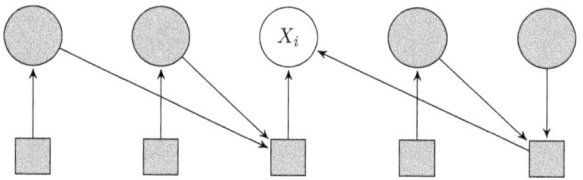

Figure 2.5: Message passing scheme for computing $P(X_i)$.

other than the recipient:

$$m_{X_i \to F_j}(X_i) = \begin{cases} \prod_{F_k \in Ne(X_i) \setminus \{F_j\}} m_{F_k \to X_i}(X_i) & \text{if } Ne(X_i) \neq \{F_j\} \\ 1 & \text{otherwise} \end{cases}$$

A factor message from F_j to variable X_i is the product of the its factor function f_j and the variable messages coming from the neighbors other than the recipient, marginalized for every possible values of $X_1, ..., X_M \in Ne(F_j) \setminus \{X_i\}$:

$$m_{F_j \to X_i}(X_i) = \sum_{X_1} ... \sum_{X_M} f_j(X_1, ..., X_i, ..., X_M) \cdot \prod_{X_k \in Ne(F_j) \setminus \{X_i\}} m_{X_k \to F_j}(X_k)$$

The factor graph is initially oriented as a tree having X_i as a root, as shown in figure 2.5. Then, messages are sent from leaf nodes up to the parents. When X_i receives all the messages from neighboring factors $Ne(X_i)$, its marginal given the evidence is:

$$P(X_i) = \prod_{F_j \in Ne(X_i)} m_{f_j \to X_i}(X_i)$$

A similar message passing scheme, presented in section 5.3, is used in MP-MI to perform tractable inference in hybrid, tree-structured models.

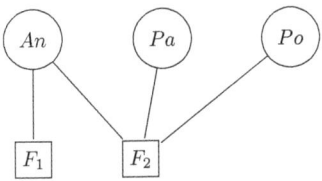

Figure 2.6: The acyclic factor graph in Example 4, corresponding to the BN in Example 1.

Example 4. Consider again the BN in Example 1. In this case, the structure does not allow the full decomposition of the joint probability into an acyclic factor graph. In order to remove the cycles, we must merge into a single factor both $f_2(An, Pa, Po) \overset{\text{def}}{=} P(Po|An, Pa) \cdot P(An|Pa)$, as depicted in figure 2.6.

Assuming variable Pa as the root, then the messages sent with the belief propagation algorithm to compute the marginal $P(Pa)$ are:

$$m_{F_1 \to An}(An) = f_1(An) = P(An)$$
$$m_{An \to F_2}(An) = m_{F_1 \to An}(An) = P(An)$$
$$m_{Po \to F_2}(Po) = 1$$
$$m_{F_2 \to Pa}(Pa) = \sum_{An} \sum_{Po} f_2(An, Pa, Po) \cdot m_{An \to F_2}(An) \cdot m_{Po \to F_2}(Po)$$
$$= \sum_{An} \sum_{Po} P(Po|An, Pa) \cdot P(Pa|An) \cdot P(An) = P(Pa)$$

Indeed, computing the marginal requires the marginalization of each other variable for computing $m_{F_2 \to Pa}$.

2.2 Inference by Weighted Model Counting

Until now, we haven't considered the problem of computing inference queries while accounting for (hard) constraints. In what follows, we will first introduce the necessary concepts in propositional logic and then generalise them to hybrid domains.

2.2.1 Propositional satisfiability

Propositional logic (PL) is the classical branch of logic that describes an algebra over propositions. A *propositional variable* (sometimes simply called *atom* or *boolean variable*) is an atomic statement that can either be *true* ($\top$) or *false* ($\bot$). Propositional formulas combine atoms by means of the usual logical operators: *negations* ($\neg$), *conjunctions* ($\wedge$), *disjunctions* ($\vee$). In what follows, we denote with $Atoms(\varphi)$ the set of atoms appearing in a logical formula φ, while we denote the *literals*, i.e. the set of the atoms and their negation, with $Literals(\varphi) \overset{\text{def}}{=} Atoms(\varphi) \cup \{\neg A \mid A \in Atoms(\varphi)\}$. Sometimes, the variables appearing in the formula are explicitly denoted in parenthesis, e.g. $\varphi(A_1, A_2)$. A *truth assignment* μ is a function that maps (a subset of) variables of a propositional formula φ to boolean values, i.e. given $A \subseteq Atoms(\varphi)$, $\mu : A \to \{\bot, \top\}$. A truth assignment is *total* when it assigns a truth value to every variable in the formula, otherwise it is called *partial*. In what follows, with a slight abuse of notation the truth assignments are represented as sets of literals corresponding to atoms in the formula, i.e. $\mu \subseteq Literals(\varphi)$. A truth assignment *satisfies* a formula φ if and only if the formula is true under that assignment, written $\mu \models \varphi$. μ is also called a *model* of φ[1]. Given a logical formula φ, let $TTA(\varphi)$ and $TA(\varphi)$ be the set of total and partial truth assignments that satisfy φ respectively. A formula φ is *satisfiable* if and only if $\exists \mu . \mu \models \varphi$, while φ is *valid* if and only if $\forall \mu . \mu \models \varphi$. The *propositional satisfiability* problem (SAT) consists in deciding whether a given formula is satisfiable[2]. Although SAT is the canonical *NP-complete* problem [22] and thus is inherently hard to solve, nowadays we can solve instances involving hundreds of thousands of variables, thanks to the theoretical and technological advancements of specialized procedures called SAT solvers. Thanks to this advancements, SAT solvers are the backend engine of many symbolic reasoning systems that are used in an enormous number of applications.

2.2.2 Weighted Model Counting

Model Counting (#SAT) is the counting analogue of the SAT decision problem. Given a propositional formula φ, the goal is to count/enumerate all its satisfying total truth assignments. More formally, the *model count* of φ is $\#\text{SAT}(\varphi) \stackrel{\text{def}}{=} |TTA(\varphi)|$.

Example 5. Consider the formula φ, which encodes the knowledge:

- *"If it rains (R) then the sky must be cloudy (C)"*

- *"The sky cannot be cloudy (C) and bright (B) at the same time"*

$$\varphi = (\neg R \vee C) \wedge \neg(C \wedge B)$$

then the set of the total truth assignments satisfying φ is:

$$TTA(\varphi) = \left\{ \begin{array}{l} \{\neg R, \neg C, \neg B\} \\ \{\neg R, \neg C, \ B\} \\ \{\neg R, \ C, \neg B\} \\ \{ \ R, \ C, \neg B\} \end{array} \right\}$$

thus, $\#\text{SAT}(\varphi) = 4$.

Many combinatorial problems can be solved by enumerating the solutions of a logical formula. In this context, every model of φ has the same relevance. In fact, no degree of uncertainty is postulated in the problem. A system that has to make decisions in a partially

---

[1] In this context, the term "model" refers to an assignment to the formula variables that satisfies it, thus it is equivalent to "satisfying truth assignment". This is not the case when we later introduce continuous numerical variables.

[2] Typically, a positive answer comes with the model that was found.

observed environment needs to reason not only about what is possible, but also about what is probable.

Weighted Model Counting (WMC) [91, 15] generalizes #SAT by assigning a weight to the models of the formula. The weight function is typically defined on the literals corresponding to the atoms appearing in the formula and the weight of a model is the product of the literals in the model.

Definition 1 (Weighted Model Count). Let φ be a propositional formula and let w be a function associating a non-negative constant weight to each literal whose atom occurs in φ, i.e.

$$w : Literals(\varphi) \to \mathbb{R}^+$$

. Then, the Weighted Model Count of φ is defined as:

$$\mathsf{WMC}(\varphi, w) \overset{\text{def}}{=} \sum_{\mu \in \mathcal{TA}(\varphi)} weight_\mu \tag{2.1}$$

$$weight_\mu \overset{\text{def}}{=} \prod_{\ell \in \mu} w(\ell)$$

The introduction of a weight function enables probabilistic reasoning, as it enables the quantification of the uncertainty on the symbolic knowledge encoded in the formula.

Example 6. Consider the following weight function, which assigns weights to $Literals(\varphi)$ from Example 5:

$$w(l) \overset{\text{def}}{=} \begin{cases} 0.2 & \text{if } l = R \\ 0.6 & \text{if } l = C \\ 1.0 & \text{otherwise} \end{cases}$$

then, the weighted model count of φ and w is:

$$\begin{aligned} \mathsf{WMC}(\varphi, w) &= [w(\neg R) \cdot w(\neg C) \cdot w(\neg B)] \\ &+ [w(\neg R) \cdot w(\neg C) \cdot w(\ B)] \\ &+ [w(\neg R) \cdot w(\ C) \cdot w(\neg B)] \\ &+ [w(\ R) \cdot w(\ C) \cdot w(\neg B)] \\ &= [1.0 \cdot 1.0 \cdot 1.0] + [1.0 \cdot 1.0 \cdot 1.0] + [1.0 \cdot 0.6 \cdot 1.0] + [0.2 \cdot 0.6 \cdot 1.0] \\ &= 2.72 \end{aligned}$$

If the weight function quantifies the degree of uncertainty on the truth values of the atoms, then the weight of each model can be interpreted as its unnormalized probability, with $\mathsf{WMC}(\varphi, w)$ being the analogue of the partition function in undirected graphical models. Thus, the pair $\langle \varphi, w \rangle$ defines a probabilistic model where w is the *unnormalized mass func-*

tion over the *support* of the distribution φ. Given two propositional formulas φ_Q and φ_E on $Atoms(\varphi)$, encoding respectively the query and evidence, the normalized conditional probability of a query Q given evidence E is computed as[3]:

$$P_{\langle \varphi, w \rangle}(Q|E) = \frac{\mathsf{WMC}(\varphi \wedge \varphi_Q \wedge \varphi_E, w)}{\mathsf{WMC}(\varphi \wedge \varphi_E, w)}$$

For instance, in the model described above, we could compute:

- *"The probability of a cloudy sky"*

$$P_{\langle \varphi, w \rangle}(C) = \frac{0.72}{2.72} \sim 0.26$$

- *"The probability that it rains **or** there's a bright sky"*

$$P_{\langle \varphi, w \rangle}(R \vee B) = \frac{1.12}{2.72} \sim 0.41$$

- *"The probability of rain **given** that the sky is not bright"*

$$P_{\langle \varphi, w \rangle}(R|\neg B) = \frac{0.12}{1.72} \sim 0.07$$

Reducing marginal inference to WMC is the state-of-the-art approach in many discrete probabilistic models. As a motivating example, we report the original reduction technique for computing conditional probability queries in discrete BNs by WMC [92]. Without loss of generality, the variables are assumed to be binary. The resulting formula φ is in CNF.

Given $\mathcal{B} = \langle \mathcal{G}, \Theta \rangle$, modelling a joint distribution over $\mathbf{X} = \{X_1, ..., X_N\}$, we need to introduce *state* and *chance* variables in our propositional theory. For each X_i, a state variable encodes its binary value [4]. In what follows, we denote the state variables with the same name as the original variables in the BN. For each CPT entry j in $P(X_i|Pa_{\mathcal{G}}(X_i)) = [\langle \mu_j, p_j \rangle]_{j=1}^{2^{|Pa_{\mathcal{G}}(X_i)|}}$, where μ_j denotes an assignment to $Pa_{\mathcal{G}}(X_i)$ and $p_j = P(X_i = \top | \mu_j)$, we add a chance variable $Ch_{X_i}^j$ with $w(Ch_{X_i}^j) = p_j$ and two clauses to φ: $(\mu_j \wedge Ch_{X_i}^j \rightarrow X_i)$ and $(\mu_j \wedge \neg Ch_{X_i}^j \rightarrow \neg X_i)$. Notice that, if the j-th entry of the CPT is deterministic, i.e. has $p_j \in \{0, 1\}$, there is no need to introduce two clauses and the chance variable. If $p_j = 0$, then the clause $(\mu_j \rightarrow \neg X_i)$ is added. If $p_j = 1$, $(\mu_j \rightarrow X_i)$ is added instead.

Example 7. Consider again the binary BN in Example 1, modelling the participation of Andrea (*An*), Paolo (*Pa*) and Pollo (*Po*) to a ML conference. Inference can be reduced to a WMC

---

[3]The definition assumes that the model conjoined with the evidence is consistent, otherwise the result is defined to be 0 to avoid the degenerate $\frac{0}{0}$ cases.

[4]As pointed out in the original paper, this is not actually needed for variables with no parents.

computation with formula:

$$\varphi = (Ch^1_{An} \to An) \wedge (\neg Ch^1_{An} \to \neg An)$$
$$\wedge (An \wedge Ch^1_{Pa} \to Pa) \wedge (An \wedge \neg Ch^1_{Pa} \to \neg Pa)$$
$$\wedge (\neg An \wedge Ch^2_{Pa} \to Pa) \wedge (\neg An \wedge \neg Ch^2_{Pa} \to \neg Pa)$$
$$\wedge (An \wedge Pa \to Po)$$
$$\wedge (An \wedge \neg Pa \wedge Ch^2_{Po} \to Po) \wedge (An \wedge \neg Pa \wedge \neg Ch^2_{Po} \to \neg Po)$$
$$\wedge (\neg An \wedge Pa \wedge Ch^3_{Po} \to Po) \wedge (\neg An \wedge Pa \wedge \neg Ch^3_{Po} \to \neg Po)$$
$$\wedge (\neg An \wedge \neg Pa \to \neg Po)$$

and weights:

$$w(Ch^1_{An}) = 0.7,$$
$$w(Ch^1_{Pa}) = 0.3, \ w(Ch^2_{Pa}) = 0.2,$$
$$w(Ch^2_{Po}) = 0.4, \ w(Ch^3_{Po}) = 0.6$$

Notice how the deterministic entries in the CPT $P(Po|An, Pa)$ are converted in hard propositional constraints.

The effectiveness of this method and the body of research in this area motivated the efforts in generalizing the techniques used in the discrete case to hybrid domains. The first step in this direction is to move from PL to more expressive languages that can represent our hybrid symbolic knowledge.

2.2.3 Logical structure

The structure of a logical problem has an effect on the computational complexity of certain tasks. For these reason, certain *normal forms* have been studied. In *conjunctive normal form* (CNF), formulas are conjunctions of clauses. Each clause is a disjunction of literals:

$$\varphi_{CNF} = \bigwedge_i \bigvee_j \ell_{i,j}$$

Disjunctive normal form (DNF) formulas are the exact opposite: i.e. the disjunction of conjunctions of literals:

$$\varphi_{DNF} = \bigvee_i \bigwedge_j \ell_{i,j}$$

Both DNF and CNF are special cases of the *negation normal form* (NNF) which only requires negations to be pushed down to the atoms. It is well known that WMC over DNF formulas admits a *fully polynomial randomized approximation scheme* (FPRAS) [46]. An FPRAS algorithm returns an approximation with statistical guarantees in polynomial time with respect to the input size, the error ϵ and the confidence δ. More formally, it returns an estimate $\hat{m}u$

of the exact solution μ such that:

$$Pr\big(\mu(1-\epsilon) \leq \hat{\mu} \leq \mu(1+\epsilon)\big) \geq 1 - \delta$$

Unfortunately, this result doesn't hold for formulas in CNF. In decision and counting problems, a popular approach is using *knowledge compilation* (KC) techniques to find a target representation of the problem that admit an efficient computation of the solution. Relevant to our purposes, it has been shown that enforcing additional properties on NNF formulas enable linear (weighted) model counting in the resulting circuit architecture. These two properties are *determinism* and decomposability. A NNF formula if decomposable if and only if each conjunct is defined on disjoint set of variables. A NNF formula is deterministic if and only if each disjunct is mutually exclusive, i.e. the conjuction of two disjunct is logically unsatisfiable. Formulas that satisfy both properties are called d-DNNF and are often used as a target representation for KC-based WMC algorithms.

2.3 Inference by Weighted Model Integration

2.3.1 Satisfiability Modulo Theories

Satisfiability Modulo Theories (SMT) generalizes SAT to theories like *uninterpreted functions with equality* ($\mathcal{EUF}$), *linear arithmetic over rationals* ($\mathcal{LRA}$), *bit-vectors* ($\mathcal{BV}$), etc. Given a theory $\mathcal{T}$, a SMT-$\mathcal{T}$ formula can contain both propositional and theory atoms. Given a SMT-$\mathcal{T}$ formula φ, the SMT problem consists in deciding whether there exists a satisfying truth assignment to its atoms. In SMT, a satisfying truth assignment has to both propositionally satisfy φ and be consistent with $\mathcal{T}$. Thanks to an effective combination of modern CDCL algorithms and specialized theory solvers, SMT found successful applications in hardware/software verification (see e.g. [20, 28]), symbolic optimization [65] and bioinformatics [69]. For a more detailed introduction on the theory and applications of SMT, see [7].

In what follows, we focus on SMT-$\mathcal{LRA}$. This language can represent complex logical and algebraic relationships between boolean variables $\mathbf{A} = \{A_1, ..., A_n\}$ and continuous variables $\mathbf{X} = \{X_1, ..., X_m\}$. Specifically, $\mathcal{LRA}$-atoms are linear equalities or inequalities between continuous variables:

$$\Big(\sum_{X_i \in \mathbf{X}} a_i \cdot X_i \bowtie b\Big) \quad \text{where } \bowtie \in \{<, \leq, >, \geq, =, \neq\}, a_i, b \in \mathbb{R}$$

We denote by $\mathcal{TTA}(\varphi) \stackrel{\text{def}}{=} \{\mu_1, ..., \mu_j, ...\}$ the set of all $\mathcal{LRA}$-satisfiable *total* truth assignments μ on $Atoms(\varphi)$ propositionally satisfying φ. $\mathcal{TTA}(\varphi)$ is unique. We denote by $\mathcal{TA}(\varphi) \stackrel{\text{def}}{=} \{\mu_1, ..., \mu_j, ...\}$ any set of $\mathcal{LRA}$-satisfiable *partial* truth assignments μ on $Atoms(\varphi)$ propositionally satisfying φ, s.t. (i) every total truth assignment $\eta \in \mathcal{TTA}(\varphi)$ is a super-assignment of one μ_j in $\mathcal{TA}(\varphi)$, and (ii) every pair μ_i, μ_j assigns opposite truth values to at least one element, i.e., $\mu_i \wedge \mu_j \models_{\mathbb{B}} \bot$ (hence $\mu_i \wedge \mu_j \models_{\mathcal{LRA}} \bot$). $\mathcal{TA}(\varphi)$ is not unique, and $\mathcal{TTA}(\varphi)$ is a particular case of $\mathcal{TA}(\varphi)$.

The disjunction of the μ's in $\mathcal{TA}(\varphi)$ is $\mathcal{LRA}$-equivalent to φ (see e.g. [95]):

$$\varphi =_{\mathcal{LRA}} \bigvee_{\mu \in \mathcal{TA}(\varphi)} \mu \qquad (2.2)$$

Example 8. Consider the SMT-$\mathcal{LRA}$ formula with $\mathbf{A} = \{faulty\}$ and $\mathbf{X} = \{temp\}$:

$$\varphi \stackrel{\text{def}}{=} ((temp < -40.0) \vee (temp > 200.0)) \rightarrow faulty$$

then:

$$\mathcal{TTA}(\varphi) = \left\{ \begin{array}{l} \{\neg(temp < -40.0), \neg(temp > 200.0), \neg faulty\} \\ \{\neg(temp < -40.0), \neg(temp > 200.0), \ faulty\} \\ \{\neg(temp < -40.0), \ (temp > 200.0), \ faulty\} \\ \{\ (temp < -40.0), \neg(temp > 200.0), \ faulty\} \end{array} \right\}$$

In this example, the assignment

$$\{(temp < -40.0), (temp > 200.0), faulty\}$$

does propositionally satisfy φ but it is not consistent with the $\mathcal{LRA}$ theory, since $temp$ cannot be at the same time smaller than -40.0 and larger than 200.0.

In contrast with SAT, the satisfying assignments or solutions of an SMT problem do not necessarily correspond to the models of the formula. In fact, when we consider continuous numbers, there might be an infinite number of models for a single solution.

In the following sections, given an assignment μ to the atoms of a SMT-$\mathcal{LRA}$ formula, we denote with $\mu^{\mathcal{LRA}}$ and $\mu^{\mathbf{A}}$ the subparts of μ regarding $\mathcal{LRA}$-atoms and propositional atoms respectively.

Example 9. Consider the SMT-$\mathcal{LRA}$ formula on variables $\mathbf{X} = \{x, y\}$, $\mathbf{A} = \{A\}$:

$$\chi \stackrel{\text{def}}{=} (0 \leq x) \wedge (0 \leq y) \wedge (y \leq 3)$$
$$\wedge (\ A \rightarrow (x \leq 2))$$
$$\wedge (\neg A \rightarrow ((0 \leq x) \wedge (x + y \leq 3)))$$

This formula defines two sub-spaces of $x \times y$ conditioned on the truth value of A, as depicted in figure 2.7.

From a representation perspective, SMT-$\mathcal{LRA}$ formulas can encode complex hybrid supports, where the projection on the continuous subspace is the union of multivariate polytopes. As in the purely discrete case, we can enable probabilistic reasoning by introducing a weight function over the solutions of an SMT problem.

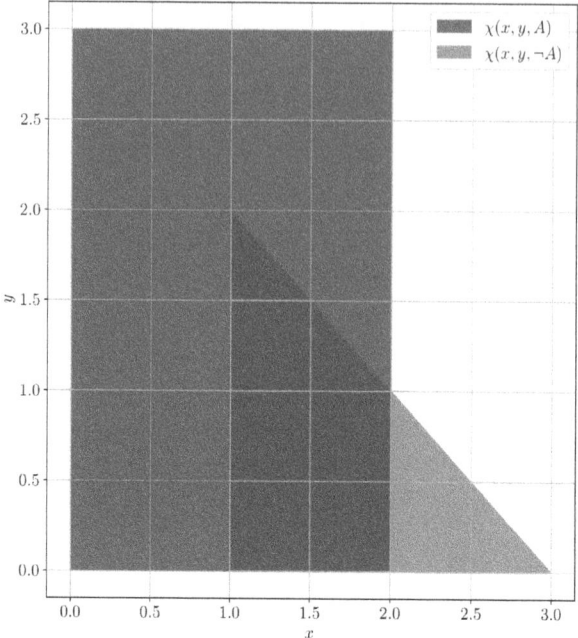

Figure 2.7: The hybrid space defined in Example 9.

2.3.1.1 Formula abbreviations

In the rest of the thesis we use the following formula abbreviations, all written in the form

$$[\![\langle expression \rangle]\!]$$

denoting the $\mathcal{LRA}$-encoding of $\langle expression \rangle$, the latter being some mathematical concept which cannot be represented as an $\mathcal{LRA}$ atom. Let t, t_i be $\mathcal{LRA}$ terms, φ, φ_i be $\mathcal{LRA}$ formulas, and $I = [l, u]$ be some interval; then

- we use "$[\![t \in I]\!]$" as a shortcut for the formula $(t \geq l) \wedge (t \leq u)$, possibly with ">" or "<" if some end of the interval is open;

- we use "$[\![\text{OneOf}\{\varphi_1, ..., \varphi_n\}]\!]$" as a shortcut for the formula $(\bigvee_{i=1}^{n} \varphi_i) \wedge \bigwedge_{1 \leq i < j \leq n} \neg(\varphi_i \wedge \varphi_j)$, i.e, exactly one φ_i holds;

- we use "$[\![\text{If } \varphi \text{ Then } t_1 \text{ Else } t_2]\!]$" to represent an if-then-else expression, that is, $t = [\![\text{If } \varphi \text{ Then } t_1 \text{ Else } t_2]\!]$ is equivalent to $(\varphi \rightarrow (t = t_1)) \wedge (\neg\varphi \rightarrow (t = t_2))$;

- we use "$[\![\text{Case } \varphi_1 : t_1; \; \varphi_2 : t_2; \; ...]\!]$" to generalize the if-then-else to the case of multiple mutually-exclusive and exhaustive conditions, that is, $t = [\![\text{Case } \varphi_1 : t_1; \; \varphi_2 : t_2; \; ...]\!]$ is equivalent to $\bigwedge_i(\varphi_i \rightarrow (t = t_i))$, under the assumption that the conditions φ_i are exhaustive –that is, $\models_{\mathcal{LRA}} \bigvee_i \varphi_i$– and mutually exclusive – that is, $\varphi_i \wedge \varphi_j \models_{\mathcal{LRA}} \bot$

for every i, j. [5]

2.3.2   Weighted Model Integration

We are now ready to introduce the core computational concept of this thesis, *Weighted Model Integration* (WMI) [10]. Intuitively, WMI generalizes WMC to hybrid domains, allowing marginalization over both continuous and discrete variables.

Definition 2 (Weighted Model Integral). Let φ be a SMT-$\mathcal{LRA}$ formula on the set of continuous variables $\mathbf{X}$ and Boolean variables $\mathbf{A}$. Let $w(\ell, \mathbf{X})$ be a function associating an expression on $\mathbf{X}$ to $Literals(\varphi)$. The Weighted Model Integral of φ is defined as:

$$\mathsf{WMI}(\varphi, w) \stackrel{\text{def}}{=} \sum_{\mu \in \mathcal{TA}(\varphi)} \int_{\mu^{\mathcal{LRA}}} weight_\mu(\mathbf{X}) \, d\mathbf{X} \tag{2.3}$$

$$weight_\mu(\mathbf{X}) \stackrel{\text{def}}{=} \prod_{\ell \in \mu} w(\ell, \mathbf{X})$$

Again, the weight factorizes according to $Literals(\varphi)$ [6] but, contrarily to the discrete case, the potential associated with a literal is not necessarily constant. Another difference with respect to WMC is that, due to the introduction of continuous variables, we might have infinite models for each satisfying truth assignment μ. For this reason, we need to integrate $weight_\mu(\mathbf{X})$ over the subspace defined by $\mu^{\mathcal{LRA}}$. While in principle the definition above holds for *nonlinear arithmetic over rationals* (SMT-$\mathcal{NRA}$), most of the reasearch efforts have focused on SMT-$\mathcal{LRA}$ constraints due to the additional computational complexity of the non-linear case. Throughout this thesis we will thus restrict to linear constraints. Regarding the weight function expressions, most works use multivariate polynomials on $\mathbf{X}$, although exceptions do exist (e.g. [70, 111]). Piecewise polynomials have some useful properties:

- they can arbitrarily approximate any density function;

- they are closed under sum, product and integration;

- there exist both numerical and symbolic procedures for integrating (piecewise) polynomials over convex polytopes [6].

Notice that, in order to have a well-defined WMI, the densities $weight_\mu(\mathbf{X})$ have to be non-negative for every assignment to $\mathbf{X}$ that is consistent with μ.

---

[5]Note that the mutual exclusion guarantes that the semantics of $[\![\mathsf{Case}\ \varphi_1 : t_1;\ \varphi_2 : t_2;\ ...]\!]$ is not sequential, and it does not depend on the order of the conditions $\varphi_1, \varphi_2, ...$

[6]While this is an intuitive generalization of the WMC definition in Def. 1 to the hybrid case, an alternative formulation will be later introduced in chapter 4 to accommodate the theory behind the improved algorithm presented there.

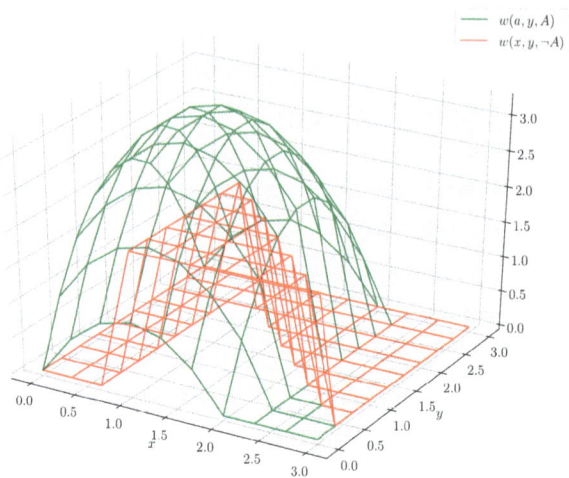

Figure 2.8: The unnormalized density defined in Example 10.

Example 10. Consider the formula χ from 9 and the following weight function:

$$w(\ell, x, y) \stackrel{\text{def}}{=} \begin{cases} -x^2 - y^2 + 2x + 3y & \text{if } \ell = A \\ -2x - 2y + 6 & \text{if } \ell = \neg A \\ 1.0 & \text{otherwise} \end{cases}$$

Since $w(\ell, x, y) = 1 \; \forall \ell \notin \{A, \neg A\}$, the weight function encodes two mutually exclusive cases conditioned on the truth value of A, as depicted in figure 2.8.

Analogously to the discrete case, probabilistic inference in hybrid probabilistic models can be reduced to WMI. The pair $\langle \varphi, w \rangle$ defines a probabilistic model where w is the *unnormalized density function* over the *support* of the distribution φ. Given two SMT-$\mathcal{LRA}$ formulas φ_Q and φ_E on $Atoms(\varphi)$, encoding respectively the query and evidence, the normalized conditional probability of a query Q given evidence E is computed as[7]:

$$P_{\langle \varphi, w \rangle}(Q|E) = \frac{\text{WMI}(\varphi \wedge \varphi_Q \wedge \varphi_E, w)}{\text{WMI}(\varphi \wedge \varphi_E, w)}$$

Example 11. Consider the SMT-$\mathcal{LRA}$ formula on $\mathbf{X} = \{x\}$ and $\mathbf{A} = \{A_1, A_2, A_3\}$:

$$\begin{aligned} \varphi \stackrel{\text{def}}{=} & (1 \leq x) \wedge (x \leq 5) \\ & \wedge (A_1 \leftrightarrow (\neg A_2 \wedge \neg A_3)) \\ & \wedge (A_2 \rightarrow ((1 \leq x) \wedge (x \leq 3))) \\ & \wedge (A_3 \rightarrow (\neg(x \leq 3) \wedge (x \leq 5))) \end{aligned}$$

---

[7]As in WMC, the definition assumes that the model conjoined with the evidence is consistent, otherwise the result is defined to be 0.

Let the weights of all literals be 1 except for $w(A_1) \overset{\text{def}}{=} 0.1$, $w(A_2) \overset{\text{def}}{=} 0.25 \cdot x - 0.25$ and $w(A_3) \overset{\text{def}}{=} 1.25 - 0.25 \cdot x$. First, it is easy to see that:

$$
TTA(\varphi) = \left\{
\begin{array}{l}
\{ \ A_1, \neg A_2, \neg A_3, \ (1 \le x), \ (x \le 5), \ (x \le 3)\} \\
\{ \ A_1, \neg A_2, \neg A_3, \ (1 \le x), \ (x \le 5), \neg(x \le 3)\} \\
\{\neg A_1, \ A_2, \neg A_3, \ (1 \le x), \ (x \le 5), \ (x \le 3)\} \\
\{\neg A_1, \neg A_2, \ A_3, \ (1 \le x), \ (x \le 5), \neg(x \le 3)\}
\end{array}
\right\}
$$

then, we have[8]:

$$
\text{WMI}(\varphi, w) = \int_{(1 \le x) \wedge (x \le 5) \wedge (x \le 3)} w(A_1) \, dx + \int_{(1 \le x) \wedge (x \le 5) \wedge \neg(x \le 3)} w(A_1) \, dx
$$

$$
+ \int_{(1 \le x) \wedge (x \le 5) \wedge (x \le 3)} w(A_2) \, dx + \int_{(1 \le x) \wedge (x \le 5) \wedge \neg(x \le 3)} w(A_3) \, dx
$$

$$
= \int_{[1,3]} 0.1 dx + \int_{(3,5]} 0.1 \, dx
$$

$$
+ \int_{[1,3]} 0.25 \cdot x - 0.25 \, dx + \int_{(3,5]} 1.25 - 0.25 \cdot x \, dx
$$

$$
= [0.1 \cdot x]_1^3 + [0.1 \cdot x]_3^5
$$

$$
+ \left[0.125 \cdot x^2 - 0.25 \cdot x\right]_1^3 + \left[1.25 \cdot x - 0.125 \cdot x^2\right]_3^5
$$

$$
= 0.3 - 0.1 + 0.5 - 0.3 + 0.375 + 0.125 + 3.125 - 2.625 = 1.4
$$

This example models an unnormalized distribution over x ranging from one to five, which is uniform if A_1 is true, and is modeled as a triangular distribution with mode at $x = 3$ otherwise. Again, $\text{WMI}(\varphi, w)$ is the partition function constant. Suppose that we are interested in computing the probability that $x \le 2$ (query), given the unnormalized distribution represented by $\langle \varphi, w \rangle$ pair and the information that $A_1 = \bot$ (evidence). This probability can be computed as:

$$
P_{\langle \varphi, w \rangle}(x \le 2 | A_1 = \bot) = \frac{\text{WMI}(\varphi \wedge \neg A_1 \wedge (x \le 2), w)}{\text{WMI}(\varphi \wedge \neg A_1, w)} = \frac{0.125}{1.0} = 0.125
$$

because:

$$
\text{WMI}(\varphi \wedge \neg A_1, w) = \int_{(1 \le x) \wedge (x \le 5) \wedge (x \le 3)} w(A_2) \, dx
$$

$$
+ \int_{(1 \le x) \wedge (x \le 5) \wedge \neg(x \le 3)} w(A_3) \, dx
$$

$$
= \int_{[1,3]} 0.25 \cdot x - 0.25 \, dx + \int_{(3,5]} 1.25 - 0.25 \cdot x \, dx
$$

$$
= \left[0.125 \cdot x^2 - 0.25 \cdot x\right]_1^3 + \left[1.25 \cdot x - 0.125 \cdot x^2\right]_3^5
$$

$$
= 0.375 + 0.125 + 3.125 - 2.625 = 1.0
$$

---

[8]For better readability, we drop from products the weights $w(\ell)$ which are equal to 1.

$$\text{WMI}(\varphi \wedge \neg A_1 \wedge (x \leq 2), w) = \int_{(1 \leq x) \wedge (x \leq 5) \wedge (x \leq 3) \wedge (x \leq 2)} w(A_2) \, dx$$

$$= \int_{[1,2]} 0.25 \cdot x - 0.25 \, dx$$

$$= \left[0.125 \cdot x^2 - 0.25 \cdot x \right]_1^2$$

$$= 0.0 + 0.125 = 0.125$$

Remark 1. The main motivation behind the introduction of WMI was that of enabling probabilistic inference in hybrid domains. In that scenario, it was implicitly assumed that a pair $\langle \varphi, w \rangle$ defines the unnormalized distribution, and that any additional formula representing evidence or queries does not introduce any additional Boolean or continuous variables with respect to those in φ, and that the weight of any literal of atoms not in φ has a constant weight of 1. The alternative formulation introduced in section 4.2 is more explicit in that sense.

CHAPTER 3

RELATED WORK

3.1 Modelling and inference

Conditional Gaussian (CG) models are the first formalism that was proposed for modelling hybrid domains [60, 61]. Originally, in order to support exact inference, discrete variables could not be conditioned on continuous ones. This requirement is quite restrictive, for instance it doesn't allow modelling a fire alarm triggered by smoke concentration, or a thermostat. Conditional Linear Gaussian (CLG) models were extended with logit or probit distributions, thus supporting discrete variables with continuous parents at the cost of approximating the local computations with variational inference [79] or Gaussian quadrature [63].

Discretization is a well-studied approach to hybrid modelling [27, 18] and is widely adopted in applications where distributional assumptions cannot be made. Specific discretization techniques in the context of BNs were also proposed [32, 55, 80]. A drawback of discretization is that the algebraic relationships between variables are lost. Moreover, approximating a continuous distribution with piecewise constant densities is often prohibitive in high dimensions or results in poor accuracy. Non-uniform discretization mitigates this problem but is still problematic for variables whose posterior marginal depends on the evidence of related variables.

An alternative representation involves mixtures of truncated exponentials (MTEs) [75, 21], which generalize the piecewise constant approximations used for discretization with piecewise exponentials. Although easy to integrate, MTEs are difficult to estimate from data as it requires solving non-linear optimization problems. Mixtures of polynomials (MOPs) [98] were proposed as an easier-to-estimate alternative to MTEs. MOP approximations of a differentiable PDF can be found by considering its Taylor series expansion or by using Lagrange interpolation. As for MTEs, multi-dimensional MOPs were originally defined over axis-aligned hypercubes and thus couldn't easily capture deterministic multivariate relationships. This limitation was removed by allowing MOPs to be defined over hyper-rhombuses [96], hitting the middle-ground between axis-aligned hypercubes and arbitrary polytopes. Mixtures of truncated basis functions (MTBFs) [58] unify MTEs and MOPs by observing that potentials in the two representations differ in the type of core functions while sharing the same structure. Finally, [108] generalize undirected Generalized Linear Models [107] to hybrid domains.

Although BNs and similar formalisms were extended to hybrid domains, they are typically more suited for modelling uncertainty rather than deterministic relations. Statistical Relational Learning (SRL) [54] is an active area devoted to designing probabilistic models for structured, relational domains. While SRL models are typically restricted to discrete settings, there has been a growing interest in designing hybrid SRL formalisms, such as Hybrid Markov Logic Networks (HMLNs) [103] or Hybrid Problog (HPB) [41]. Constraints pose additional challenges for inference and special purpose algorithms must be devised to deal with the deterministic structure effectively [25, 59]. Scalability is obtained by either restricting the expressivity of the underlying formalism, or by resorting to approximate inference.

Traditional Markov Chain Monte Carlo (MCMC) [36] techniques can be readily applied in the hybrid case, but they typically struggle when the support of the distribution is highly structured, as the convergence rate is prohibitive due to rejection. Sampling approaches that account for the constrained structure of the problem were proposed for purely discrete settings setting [37, 38, 14], for hybrid probabilistic programs [104, 105] and for hybrid probabilistic models with mixed propositional and piecewise polynomial potentials [3, 2, 4].

Extended Algebraic Decision Diagrams (XADDs) [94] were introduced in the context of hybrid planning to compactly encode the value function of a broad class of discrete/continuous Markov Decision Processes (DC-MDPs). The same data structure was later used in Symbolic Variable Elimination (SVE) [93], an exact probabilistic inference algorithm for piecewise polynomial factor graphs (PPFGs). The PPFG formalism is equivalent to WMI. In fact, XADDs were recently considered as a compilation language for solving WMI problems [50].

Closest to SVE is Probabilistic Inference Modulo Theories [112] (PIMT), a symbolic framework where a combination of DPLL and variable elimination is used to solve inference problems on a variety of theories. While initially focused on integer arithmetic, the system developed by the authors (called PRAiSE) was later extended with support for arithmetic over the reals and polynomial densities. In contrast with SVE, PRAiSE directly operates on the symbolic representation of the problem rather than compiling a circuit.

The PSI solver [35] is a flexible symbolic inference engine for hybrid continuous/discrete probabilistic programs that can be used to compute exact inference for many classes of hybrid probabilistic models, although it lacks an efficient support for combinatorial reasoning and thus is not indicated for probabilistic models with a complex logical structure.

Exact algorithms for WMI usually fall in two categories (with some exceptions mentioned in the following): *solver-based* and *circuit-based algorithms*. The former approach decomposes the problem in two steps: first, the combinatorial enumeration of the satisfying truth assignments is delegated to a specialized SMT solver, then the integration of the solutions is performed either by numerical or symbolic procedures. The latter approach leverages compact representations of the problem (often in conjunction with knowledge compilation techniques) to reduce inference to a series of repeated symbolic operations on the data structure. The first algorithms that explicitly solved WMI problems [10] were based on SMT solvers and either relied on a block clause[1] strategy (WMI-BC) or more advanced SMT features like parallel enumeration of all solutions (WMI-ALLSMT).

In the propositional (WMC) case, substantial efficiency gains can be obtained by leveraging component caching techniques [90, 5], in which the weighted model counts of disjoint components of a formula are cached once and reused whenever the formula is encountered again in the computation. Unfortunately, these strategies are difficult to apply in the WMI case, because of the additional coupling induced by algebraic constraints. A recent work [8] did show substantial computational savings in adapting #DPLL with component caching from the WMC to the WMI case. The approach however works with purely piecewise polynomial densities, with no additional constraints between theory variables. In this setting, the reasoning part boils down to plain SAT, and an eager encoding of the piecewise structure allows to apply component caching at the propositional level and leave the integration of densities to the final steps of the decomposition procedure. Albeit effective, this solution cannot be applied whenever algebraic constraints exist between variables, e.g. their sum being within a certain range, a rather common situation in many practical cases (see section 4.3).

By recognizing that the partial symbolic marginalization computed on an XADD results in a parameterized WMI computation, a symbolic dynamic programming algorithm [50] was proposed. The resulting solver overcomes the limitation of SVE by caching intermediate results and thus exploit the DAG structure of the compiled XADD. Moreover, the solver can compute partial WMI problems and supports integer variables.

The unique approach of Search-based MI (SMI) [109] consists in reducing the WMI problem to MI, as described in section 5.1. Then, the problem of computing the volume in the full continuous space is reduced to finding an equivalent univariate piecewise integral. This step leverages context-specific independence to perform an efficient search of the bounds and degrees of the integrands involved in the univariate integration. Finally, each of the actual integrands can be recovered by polynomial interpolation inside the corresponding bounds and the integral can be computed efficiently in the number of pieces. The search-based procedure in the dependency structure of the problem later inspired the algorithmic ideas presented in chapter 5.

Approximate WMI inference is a less explored field. The first approximate algorithm for WMI [9] leverages hashing-based sampling techniques that has proven effective in WMC [14, 29]. Contrarily to the discrete case, the probabilistic guarantees on the error bounds do not hold in the general hybrid scenario. Knowledge compilation is used in [111] to compactly represent the combinatorial structure of WMI problems. The compiled problem can then be solved either by exact symbolic integration using the PSI solver [35], or by computing a Monte Carlo approximation with the Edward library [101]. This approach has the benefit of supporting non-linear constraints and probability density functions.

---

[1] The solver is iteratively called on the original formula conjoined with the negation of previously found solutions.

3.2 Learning

Learning in hybrid domains hasn't received as much attention as the purely discrete and purely continuous cases. In the context of hybrid BNs, the structure can be learned on discretized data, using the original hybrid data for parameter estimation as proposed in [73]. Algorithms for structure and parameter learning were proposed for hybrid BNs with MTE potentials [88, 74], undirected Manichean graphical models [108].

Most works for learning hybrid SRL models assume a given structure, focusing on parameter learning. Learner of Local Models (LLM) [87] is an approach for learning the structure of hybrid Relational Dependency Networks. [81] leverages LLM in order to learn the state transition model of hybrid relational MDPs, expressed in the language of Dynamic Distributional Clauses.

The seminal work on WMI [10] covers maximum likelihood estimation of piecewise constant densities, assuming that both the support and the piecewise structure of the density is given.

Finding the support of a WMI distribution is a constraint learning problem. A discussion of the different aspects of the problem, as well as an extensive survey of the existing approaches, is presented in to [85]. An algorithm for learning SMT-$\mathcal{LRA}$ constraints from labelled data is presented in [52].

Weight learning in WMI is closely related to non-parametric multivariate density estimation, a venerable field of study. Textbook approaches include histograms [30] and kernel density estimation (KDE) [40]. Histograms partition the space into regularly sized bins, each associated to a constant density. Adaptive histograms fit a local regressor (e.g., a spline) at each bin to capture the finer details while allowing the bin size to grow adaptively [44]. KDE fits a local density around each data point. The runtime of these methods grows quickly with the number of dimensions and/or data points. Multivariate adaptive regression splines (MARS) [31] is another classical, greedy space-partitioning model (with polynomial leaves) that tends to be more efficient than histograms and KDE.

Recently, more efficient tree- and grid-based approaches have been introduced to address the efficiency issues of classical methods. Tree-based methods [64, 71] such as Density Estimation Trees (DETs) [86] achieve considerable scalability by recursively partitioning the space based on axis-aligned splits. The splits are obtained in an adaptive manner by greedily optimizing the integrated square error. Notably, DETs support hybrid domains. Grid-based methods [83] recursively partition the space too, but they place the splits at fixed, progressively finer-grained locations.

In the discrete case, learning of structured distributions has been explored for probabilistic sentential decision diagrams [48] from both examples and pre-specified constraints [66]. These techniques, however, have not been extended to hybrid domains. On the other hand, MSPNs [72] are state-of-the-art density estimators that extend Sum-Product Networks [84] by introducing continuous variables and polynomial densities at the leaves. Like DETs, MSPNs allow efficient inference so long as the query formula is axis-aligned, and are learned using a greedy scheme. DETs and MSPNs will be discussed in detail later on. Hybrid SPNs [12] is another very recent alternative and could be used in place of MPSNs.

None of the above models can learn or represent structured, oblique supports, which are crucial in many applications, including safety-critical ones. As the experimental evaluation in section 6.2 highlights, taking the support into account can lead to dramatically improved performance in some applications.

CHAPTER 4

WMI-PA

We begin this chapter with an example that motivated our work on improving the existing solver-based algorithms.

Example 12. Consider the WMI distribution over x, y depicted in figure 4.1 (left), where the two disjoined regions are characterized by different densities f_1 and f_2. The change in the weight depends on whether $(x > \frac{1}{2})$. The support of the distribution is encoded by the formula

$$\chi(x, y) = (0 \leq x) \wedge (x \leq 1) \wedge (0 \leq y) \wedge (y \leq 1)$$
$$\wedge ((x > \frac{1}{2}) \rightarrow (y > \frac{1}{3}))$$
$$\wedge (\neg(x > \frac{1}{2}) \rightarrow (y < \frac{2}{3}))$$

and the weight function associates $f_1(x, y)$ and $f_2(x, y)$ to the literals $(x > \frac{1}{2})$ and $\neg(x > \frac{1}{2})$ respectively. In order to compute the weighted model integral, we need to enumerate all total truth assignments of $Atoms(\chi)$, i.e.:

$$\mu_1 = \{ \ (0 \leq x), \ (x \leq 1), \ (0 \leq y), \ (y \leq 1), \neg(x > \frac{1}{2}), \ (y > \frac{1}{3}), \ (y < \frac{2}{3})\}$$
$$\mu_2 = \{ \ (0 \leq x), \ (x \leq 1), \ (0 \leq y), \ (y \leq 1), \neg(x > \frac{1}{2}), \neg(y > \frac{1}{3}), \ (y < \frac{2}{3})\}$$
$$\mu_3 = \{ \ (0 \leq x), \ (x \leq 1), \ (0 \leq y), \ (y \leq 1), \ (x > \frac{1}{2}), \ (y > \frac{1}{3}), \neg(y < \frac{2}{3})\}$$
$$\mu_4 = \{ \ (0 \leq x), \ (x \leq 1), \ (0 \leq y), \ (y \leq 1), \ (x > \frac{1}{2}), \ (y > \frac{1}{3}), \ (y < \frac{2}{3})\}$$

Notice however that μ_1 and μ_2 share the same integrand and that their conjunction is convex, and the same applies for μ_3 and μ_4, as depicted in figure 4.1 (right). In principle, the WMI could be computed with 2 integrations if it were possible to enumerate the truth assignments of the relevant atoms only.

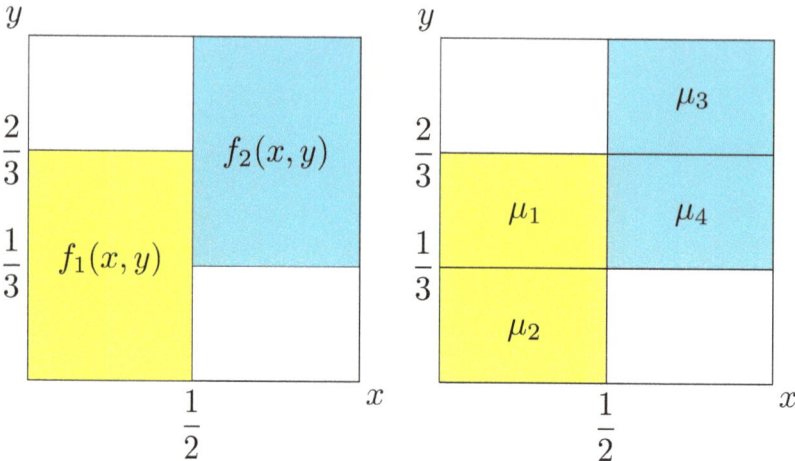

Figure 4.1: Left: the distribution in example 12, whose support is encoded as $\chi(x, y) = (0 \leq x) \wedge (x \leq 1) \wedge (0 \leq y) \wedge (y \leq 1) \wedge ((x > \frac{1}{2}) \rightarrow (y > \frac{1}{3})) \wedge (\neg(x > \frac{1}{2}) \rightarrow (y < \frac{2}{3}))$. Right: the partitioning induced by enumerating all total truth assignment of $Atoms(\chi)$, as done by the existing solver-based WMI algorithms.

Numerical integration, is a computationally demanding procedure. In fact, integrating a polynomial over a convex polytope is a #P-hard problem [6]. Avoiding needless integrations is thus crucial for solving WMI exactly.

Abstraction is a fundamental notion in automated reasoning and formal verification. Intuitively, abstraction enables reasoning over a set of predicates of interest without explicitly reasoning over the full model. We rely on the notion of *predicate abstraction* [39], a widely used technique in hybrid verification that enables reasoning over finite-state abstractions of systems with potentially infinite state spaces [39, 57, 13]. In our context, these predicates are the conditions that define how the density changes over the support. In the original definition of WMI, the weight function is a map from literals to polynomial expressions and the unnormalized density in the different regions is the product of (subsets of) these expressions. In order to fully leverage abstraction techniques in WMI, a more structured formulation for the weight function must be introduced.

These considerations led to WMI-PA, an exact solver-based algorithm that efficiently performs combinatorial reasoning while abstracting from the full $\mathcal{LRA}$ theory. This technique drastically reduces the number of integrations performed by the existing solver-based approaches, with huge performance gains in computing probabilistic queries.

Section 4.1 formally introduces predicate abstraction, followed by the alternative formulation described in section 4.2. For clarity, in the following the original definition in 2.3 is dubbed WMI$_{old}$. Section 4.3 presents a real-world case study that further motivates the introduction of the alternative formulation. Our algorithm, WMI-PA, is described in section 4.4. Finally, section 4.5 reports an empirical evaluation of the performance on both synthetic and real world benchmarks.

4.1 Predicate Abstraction

The core concept behind the inference algorithm described in this chapter is *predicate abstraction*. The intuition is that, in many applications, it is more practical to reason over a set of formulas or properties (called predicates) that abstract the behaviour of a much more complex system.

Definition 3. Let

- φ be a $\mathcal{LRA}$-formula on $\mathbf{X}$ and $\mathbf{A}$;

- $\mathbf{\Psi} \overset{\text{def}}{=} \{\psi_1, ..., \psi_K\}$ be a set of $\mathcal{LRA}$-formulas over $\mathbf{X}$ and $\mathbf{A}$;

- $\mathbf{B} \overset{\text{def}}{=} \{B_1, ..., B_K\}$ be a set of fresh atomic propositions s.t. $\mathbf{A} \cap \mathbf{B} = \varnothing$.

Then we call a **Predicate Abstraction** of φ with respect to $\mathbf{\Psi}$ on $\mathbf{B}$, namely $\mathsf{PredAbs}_{[\varphi, \mathbf{\Psi}]}(\mathbf{B})$, any propositional formula equivalent to the formula

$$\exists \mathbf{A} \exists \mathbf{X}. \left(\varphi(\mathbf{X}, \mathbf{A}) \wedge \bigwedge_{k=1}^{K} (B_k \iff \psi_k(\mathbf{X}, \mathbf{A})) \right). \tag{4.1}$$

We define $\mathsf{PredAbs}_{[\varphi]}(\mathbf{\Psi}) \overset{\text{def}}{=} \mathsf{PredAbs}_{[\varphi, \mathbf{\Psi}]}(\mathbf{B})[\mathbf{B} \leftarrow \mathbf{\Psi}]$, that is, the $\mathcal{LRA}$-formula obtained from the propositional formula $\mathsf{PredAbs}_{[\varphi, \mathbf{\Psi}]}(\mathbf{B})$ by substituting each B_k with its corresponding ψ_k.

Note that in definition 3 the formulas ψ_k are neither necessarily atomic, nor necessarily sub-formulas of φ. $\mathsf{PredAbs}_{[\varphi, \mathbf{\Psi}]}(\mathbf{B})$ defines an equivalence class of propositional formulas over $\mathbf{B}$, i.e., (4.1) may represent many syntactically-different albeit logically-equivalent propositional formulas.

Example 13. Consider the formula on variables $\mathbf{A} \overset{\text{def}}{=} \{A_1\}$ and $\mathbf{X} \overset{\text{def}}{=} \{x_1, x_2\}$:

$$\varphi \overset{\text{def}}{=} A_1 \wedge (x_1 + x_2 > 12)$$

and assume that we are interested in the predicates:

$$\psi_1 \overset{\text{def}}{=} (x_1 + x_2 = 2)$$
$$\psi_2 \overset{\text{def}}{=} (x_1 - x_2 < 10)$$

Then we have that:

$$\mathsf{PredAbs}_{[\varphi,\Psi]}(\mathbf{B}) \;=\; \exists A_1.\exists x_1 x_2. \begin{pmatrix} A_1 \wedge (x_1 + x_2 > 12)\wedge \\ (B_1 \iff (x_1 + x_2 = 2))\wedge \\ (B_2 \iff (x_1 - x_2 < 10)) \end{pmatrix} \qquad (4.2)$$

$$= \;(\neg B_1 \wedge \neg B_2) \vee (\neg B_1 \wedge B_2) \qquad\qquad\qquad (4.3)$$

$$= \;\neg B_1. \qquad\qquad\qquad\qquad\qquad\qquad (4.4)$$

$$\mathsf{PredAbs}_{[\varphi]}(\Psi) \;=\; \begin{array}{l} (\neg(x_1 + x_2 = 2) \wedge \neg(x_1 - x_2 < 10)) \vee \\ (\neg(x_1 + x_2 = 2) \wedge (x_1 - x_2 < 10)) \end{array} \qquad (4.5)$$

$$= \;\neg(x_1 + x_2 = 2). \qquad\qquad\qquad\qquad\qquad (4.6)$$

Note that both the equivalent propositional formulas (4.3) and (4.4) match the definition of $\mathsf{PredAbs}_{[\varphi,\Psi]}(\mathbf{B})$: (4.3) is built as the disjunction of *total* assignments on $\mathbf{B}$, whereas (4.4) is built as the disjunction of *partial* ones s.t.:

$$\mathit{TTA}(\mathsf{PredAbs}_{[\varphi,\Psi]}(\mathbf{B})) \;=\; \{(\neg B_1 \wedge \neg B_2),(\neg B_1 \wedge B_2)\} \qquad (4.7)$$

$$\mathit{TA}(\mathsf{PredAbs}_{[\varphi,\Psi]}(\mathbf{B})) \;=\; \{(\neg B_1)\} \qquad\qquad\qquad\qquad (4.8)$$

$$\mathit{TTA}(\mathsf{PredAbs}_{[\varphi]}(\Psi)) \;=\; \left\{ \begin{array}{l} (\neg(x_1 + x_2 = 2) \wedge \neg(x_1 - x_2 < 10)), \\ (\neg(x_1 + x_2 = 2) \wedge (x_1 - x_2 < 10)) \end{array} \right\} \qquad (4.9)$$

$$\mathit{TA}(\mathsf{PredAbs}_{[\varphi]}(\Psi)) \;=\; \{(\neg(x_1 + x_2 = 2))\} \qquad\qquad\qquad (4.10)$$

Note also that the other two total assignments, $B_1 \wedge B_2$ and $B_1 \wedge \neg B_2$, do not occur in (4.3) because they would both force the formula to be $\mathcal{LRA}$-unsatisfiable because of the contradictory conjuncts $(x_1 + x_2 > 12) \wedge (x_1 + x_2 = 2)$. This example highlights the potential benefits in terms of compactness when predicate abstraction is used.

It is worth noticing a few facts about predicate abstraction:

1. If Ψ is $\mathbf{A}$, then $\mathsf{PredAbs}_{[\varphi]}(\mathbf{A})$ reduces to $\exists \mathbf{X}.\varphi(\mathbf{X}, \mathbf{A})$.

2. If Ψ is $Atoms(\varphi)$, then $\mathsf{PredAbs}_{[\varphi]}(Atoms(\varphi))$ is equivalent to φ.
   Therefore $\mathit{TTA}(\mathsf{PredAbs}_{[\varphi]}(Atoms(\varphi)))$ [resp. $\mathit{TA}(\mathsf{PredAbs}_{[\varphi]}(Atoms(\varphi)))$ if and only if we admit partial assignments] is the same as $\mathit{TTA}(\varphi)$ [resp. $\mathit{TA}(\varphi)$], that is, AllSMT(φ).

3. If $\Psi \subset Atoms(\varphi)$ and $|\Psi|$ is significantly smaller than $|Atoms(\varphi)|$, then typically $|\mathit{TTA}(\mathsf{PredAbs}_{[\varphi]}(\Psi))| \ll |\mathit{TTA}(\varphi)|$.

In formal verification it is common to verify an abstraction of an otherwise intractable system. Finding a suitable abstraction requires multiple calls to a decision oracle, thus specialized procedures for the task are highly desirable.

Fortunately, very effective SMT-based techniques for computing $\mathit{TTA}(\mathsf{PredAbs}_{[\varphi,\Psi]}(\mathbf{B}))$ — and hence for $\mathit{TTA}(\mathsf{PredAbs}_{[\varphi]}(\Psi))$ — have been proposed in the literature (e.g. [57, 13]) and are implemented in modern SMT solvers like MATHSAT5 [19]. Very importantly for our purposes, these techniques work by iteratively producing a set of propositional truth assignments on $\mathbf{B}$, which are then disjoined as in (2.2). Therefore, MATHSAT5 computes

$\mathsf{PredAbs}_{[\varphi,\boldsymbol{\Psi}]}(\mathbf{B})$ directly in the form $\mathcal{TTA}(\mathsf{PredAbs}_{[\varphi,\boldsymbol{\Psi}]}(\mathbf{B}))$ [resp. $\mathsf{PredAbs}_{[\varphi]}(\boldsymbol{\Psi})$ in the form $\mathcal{TTA}(\mathsf{PredAbs}_{[\varphi]}(\boldsymbol{\Psi}))$].

In particular MATHSAT5, on demand, can produce either the set of *total* assignments on $\mathbf{B}$, $\mathcal{TTA}(\mathsf{PredAbs}_{[\varphi,\boldsymbol{\Psi}]}(\mathbf{B}))$, or a set of *partial* ones, $\mathcal{TA}(\mathsf{PredAbs}_{[\varphi,\boldsymbol{\Psi}]}(\mathbf{B}))$, by means of assignment-reduction techniques. To this extent, we recall that MATHSAT5 does not provide an explicit command for AllSMT(φ); rather, the user has to set explicitly the definitions $\bigwedge_k (B_k \Longleftrightarrow \psi_k)$ and specify the (sub)set of $\mathbf{B}$ of interest.

4.2   Weighted Model Integration, Revisited

Definition 2 is a very direct and intuitive generalization of WMC to the hybrid case. However, it is very abstract and directly turning it into a computational procedure, as was done in all previous implementations [10, 9, 8], can result in major inefficiencies.

In the following we present a revised formulation of WMI that:

- easily captures the previous definition;

- decouples the specification of the formula and of the weight function from that of the variables on which WMI is to be computed, removing all implicit assumptions of the original formulation (see remark 1);

- is not restricted to weight functions in the form of products of weights *over literals*, but allows for much more general forms (4.2.3). This gives a remarkable flexibility in designing efficient encodings for hybrid domains, as shown with the case study on modelling journey times on road networks (4.3);

- makes it easier to develop algorithms for WMI computation that fully exploit the potential advantage of advanced SMT techniques like predicate abstraction, as will be shown in 4.4.

We start by introducing a revisited and very general definition of WMI, starting from the Boolean-free case (4.2.1) and then covering the general case (4.2.2), and finally we describe a very general class of weight functions s.t. WMI is computable (4.2.3).

4.2.1   Basic case: WMI **Without Atomic Propositions**

We investigate first the simple case where no atomic proposition comes into play. Let $\mathbf{X} \overset{\text{def}}{=} \{x_1, ..., x_N\} \in \mathbb{R}^N$. We consider a *generic* total weight function $w(\mathbf{X})$ s.t. $w : \mathbb{R}^N \longmapsto \mathbb{R}^+$, and $\mathcal{LRA}$ formulas $\varphi(\mathbf{X})$ s.t. $\varphi : \mathbb{R}^N \longmapsto \mathbb{B}$.

Definition 4. Assume φ does not contain atomic propositions and $w : \mathbb{R}^N \longmapsto \mathbb{R}^+$. Then we define the **Weighted Model Integral** of w over φ on $\mathbf{X}$ as:

$$\mathsf{WMI}_{\mathsf{nb}}(\varphi, w | \mathbf{X}) \overset{\text{def}}{=} \int_{\varphi(\mathbf{X})} w(\mathbf{X}) d\mathbf{X}, \qquad (4.11)$$

"$_{nb}$" meaning "no-Booleans", that is, as the integral of $w(\mathbf{X})$ over the set $\{\mathbf{X} \mid \varphi(\mathbf{X}) \; is \; true\}$.

The following property of $\text{WMI}_{nb}(\varphi, w|\mathbf{X})$ derives directly from definition 4.

Property 1. Given $\mathbf{X}$, w, φ, and φ' as above,

1. if φ is $\mathcal{LRA}$-unsatisfiable, then $\text{WMI}_{nb}(\varphi, w|\mathbf{X}) = 0$.

2. if $\varphi \Rightarrow_{\mathcal{LRA}} \varphi'$, then $\text{WMI}_{nb}(\varphi, w|\mathbf{X}) \leq \text{WMI}_{nb}(\varphi', w|\mathbf{X})$

3. if $\varphi \Leftrightarrow_{\mathcal{LRA}} \varphi'$, then $\text{WMI}_{nb}(\varphi, w|\mathbf{X}) = \text{WMI}_{nb}(\varphi', w|\mathbf{X})$

4. for every $\mathcal{LRA}$-formula $\psi(\mathbf{X})$,

$$\text{WMI}_{nb}(\varphi, w|\mathbf{X}) \quad = \quad \text{WMI}_{nb}(\varphi \wedge \psi, w|\mathbf{X}) + \text{WMI}_{nb}(\varphi \wedge \neg\psi, w|\mathbf{X}).$$

Remark 2. We stress the fact that in the definition of WMI_{nb} specifying the domain "$|\mathbf{X}$" is of primary importance. In fact, even if some x_n does not occur in φ,[1] $\text{WMI}_{nb}(\varphi, w|\mathbf{X}) = \int_{\mathbb{R}} \text{WMI}_{nb}(\varphi, w|\mathbf{X}\backslash\{x_n\})dx_n \neq \text{WMI}_{nb}(\varphi, w|\mathbf{X}\backslash\{x_n\})$. "$|\mathbf{X}$" defines the dimensions of the space we are integrating on, which must be stated. (E.g., integrating on volumes differs from integrating on surfaces.)

The above definition of $\text{WMI}_{nb}(\varphi, w|\mathbf{X})$ does not (yet) imply a practical technique for computing it, because "$\int_{\varphi(\mathbf{X})} ...d\mathbf{X}$" cannot be directly computed by numerical integration procedures, which typically can handle only *conjunctions* of $\mathcal{LRA}$-literals, not arbitrary Boolean combinations of them. To cope with this fact, we need decomposing φ into conjunctions of $\mathcal{LRA}$-literals. This is where $\mathcal{TTA}()$, $\mathcal{TA}()$ and the SMT-based techniques to compute them come into play, as described in the following.

The following property of $\text{WMI}_{nb}(\varphi, w|\mathbf{X})$ derives directly from the definition of $\mathcal{TTA}(\varphi)$ and $\mathcal{TA}(\varphi)$ and from (2.2), by recalling that the domains of the assignments $\mu^{\mathcal{LRA}}$ in $\mathcal{TTA}(\varphi)$ and $\mathcal{TA}(\varphi)$ are pairwise disjoint.

Proposition 1. Given $\mathbf{X}$, $w(\mathbf{X})$, $\varphi(\mathbf{X})$, $\mathcal{TTA}(\varphi)$ and $\mathcal{TA}(\varphi)$ as above,

$$\text{WMI}_{nb}(\varphi, w|\mathbf{X}) \quad = \sum_{\mu^{\mathcal{LRA}} \in \mathcal{TTA}(\varphi)} \text{WMI}_{nb}(\mu^{\mathcal{LRA}}, w|\mathbf{X}) \qquad (4.12)$$

$$= \sum_{\mu^{\mathcal{LRA}} \in \mathcal{TA}(\varphi)} \text{WMI}_{nb}(\mu^{\mathcal{LRA}}, w|\mathbf{X}). \qquad (4.13)$$

---

[1]It may be the case that x_n does not occur in φ even though w depends on x_n: e.g., w may be a Gaussian on x_n, so that no restriction on the domain of x_n is expressed by φ.

Proof. We prove only (4.13), because $\mathcal{TTA}(\varphi)$ is a subcase of $\mathcal{TA}(\varphi)$:

$$\mathsf{WMI_{nb}}(\varphi, w | \mathbf{X})$$
$$\{by\ (2.2)\} \quad = \quad \mathsf{WMI_{nb}}(\bigvee_{\mu^{\mathcal{LRA}} \in \mathcal{TA}(\varphi)} \mu^{\mathcal{LRA}}, w | \mathbf{X})$$
$$\{disjoint\ domains\ of\ the\ \mu^{\mathcal{LRA}}{}'s\} \quad = \quad \sum_{\mu^{\mathcal{LRA}} \in \mathcal{TA}(\varphi)} \mathsf{WMI_{nb}}(\mu^{\mathcal{LRA}}, w | \mathbf{X})$$

$\square$

Importantly, the $\mu^{\mathcal{LRA}}$s in both (4.12) and (4.13) are conjunctions of literals, so that $\mathsf{WMI_{nb}}(\mu^{\mathcal{LRA}}, w | \mathbf{X})$ is computable by standard integration solvers under reasonable hypotheses (e.g., w is a polynomial) which will be discussed in 4.3. Note that if (i) w is in the form of products of weights over a set of literals as in definition 2 and (ii) φ is defined only over such literals and (iii) φ contains no Boolean atom, then (4.12) corresponds to (2.3).

4.2.2   General Case: WMI With Atomic Propositions

We investigate now the general case, where atomic propositions come into play and both w and φ depend also on them. Let $\mathbf{A} \stackrel{\text{def}}{=} \{A_1, ..., A_M\} \in \mathbb{B}^M$. We consider thus a generic total weight function $w(\mathbf{X}, \mathbf{A})$ s.t. $w : \mathbb{R}^N \times \mathbb{B}^M \longmapsto \mathbb{R}^+$, and $\mathcal{LRA}$ formulas $\varphi(\mathbf{X}, \mathbf{A})$ s.t. $\varphi : \mathbb{R}^N \times \mathbb{B}^M \longmapsto \mathbb{B}$.

In what follows, $\mu^{\mathbf{A}}$ denotes a total truth assignment on $\mathbf{A}$, $\varphi_{[\mu^{\mathbf{A}}]}(\mathbf{X})$ denotes (any formula equivalent to) the formula obtained from φ by substituting every Boolean value A_i with its truth value in $\mu^{\mathbf{A}}$, and $w_{[\mu^{\mathbf{A}}]}(\mathbf{X})$ is w computed on $\mathbf{X}$ and on the truth values of $\mu^{\mathbf{A}}$. Thus, $\varphi_{[\mu^{\mathbf{A}}]} : \mathbb{R}^N \longmapsto \mathbb{B}$ and $w_{[\mu^{\mathbf{A}}]} : \mathbb{R}^N \longmapsto \mathbb{R}^+$.

Definition 5. Given $\mathbf{X}, \mathbf{A}$, the **Weighted Model Integral** of w over φ is defined as follows:

$$\mathsf{WMI}(\varphi, w | \mathbf{X}, \mathbf{A}) \stackrel{\text{def}}{=} \sum_{\mu^{\mathbf{A}} \in \mathbb{B}^M} \mathsf{WMI_{nb}}(\varphi_{[\mu^{\mathbf{A}}]}, w_{[\mu^{\mathbf{A}}]} | \mathbf{X}), \qquad (4.14)$$

where the $\mu^{\mathbf{A}}$'s are all total truth assignments on $\mathbf{A}$.

Example 14. Let

$$\varphi \stackrel{\text{def}}{=} (A \iff (x \geq 0)) \wedge (x \geq -1) \wedge (x \leq 1)$$

and

$$w(x, A) \stackrel{\text{def}}{=} [\![\text{If } A \text{ Then } x \text{ Else } - x]\!]$$

If $\mu^{\mathbf{A}} \stackrel{\text{def}}{=} \{(\neg A)\}$, then $\varphi_{[\mu^{\mathbf{A}}]} = \neg(x \geq 0) \wedge (x \geq -1) \wedge (x \leq 1)$ and $w_{[\mu^{\mathbf{A}}]} = -x$. Note that $\varphi_{[\mu^{\mathbf{A}}]}$ can be simplified into the equivalent formula $\neg(x \geq 0) \wedge (x \geq -1)$. Similarly, if

$\mu^{\mathbf{A}} \overset{\text{def}}{=} \{(A)\}$, then $\varphi_{[\mu^{\mathbf{A}}]}$ can be simplified into $(x \geq 0) \wedge (x \leq 1)$ and $w_{[\mu^{\mathbf{A}}]} = x$. Thus,

$$
\begin{aligned}
\mathsf{WMI}(\varphi, w | \mathbf{X}, \mathbf{A}) &\overset{\text{def}}{=} \mathsf{WMI}_{\mathsf{nb}}(\varphi_{[\{\neg A\}]}, w_{[\{\neg A\}]} | x) + \mathsf{WMI}_{\mathsf{nb}}(\varphi_{[\{A\}]}, w_{[\{A\}]} | x) \\
&= \int_{[-1,0)} -x dx + \int_{[0,1]} x dx \\
&= \frac{1}{2} + \frac{1}{2} = 1
\end{aligned}
$$

Note that in definition 5 the truth assignments $\mu^{\mathbf{A}}$ of practical interest are only those for which $\varphi_{[\mu^{\mathbf{A}}]}$ is $\mathcal{LRA}$-satisfiable, because for the others $\mathsf{WMI}_{\mathsf{nb}}(\varphi_{[\mu^{\mathbf{A}}]}, w_{[\mu^{\mathbf{A}}]} | \mathbf{X}) = 0$ by Property 1.1. We address this issue in 4.4.

The following property of $\mathsf{WMI}(\varphi, w | \mathbf{X}, \mathbf{A})$ derives directly from definition 5, by applying Property 1 to $w_{[\mu^{\mathbf{A}}]}$, $\varphi_{[\mu^{\mathbf{A}}]}$, $\varphi'_{[\mu^{\mathbf{A}}]}$, $(\varphi \wedge \psi)_{[\mu^{\mathbf{A}}]}$, and $(\varphi \wedge \neg\psi)_{[\mu^{\mathbf{A}}]}$, for every $\mu^{\mathbf{A}}$.

Property 2. Given $\mathbf{X}$, $\mathbf{A}$, w, φ, and φ' as above,

1. if φ is $\mathcal{LRA}$-unsatisfiable, then $\mathsf{WMI}(\varphi, w | \mathbf{X}, \mathbf{A}) = 0$.

2. if $\varphi \Rightarrow_{\mathcal{LRA}} \varphi'$, then $\mathsf{WMI}(\varphi, w | \mathbf{X}, \mathbf{A}) \leq \mathsf{WMI}(\varphi', w | \mathbf{X}, \mathbf{A})$

3. if $\varphi \Leftrightarrow_{\mathcal{LRA}} \varphi'$, then $\mathsf{WMI}(\varphi, w | \mathbf{X}, \mathbf{A}) = \mathsf{WMI}(\varphi', w | \mathbf{X}, \mathbf{A})$

4. for every $\mathcal{LRA}$-formula $\psi(\mathbf{X}, \mathbf{A})$,

$$
\mathsf{WMI}(\varphi, w | \mathbf{X}, \mathbf{A}) = \mathsf{WMI}(\varphi \wedge \psi, w | \mathbf{X}, \mathbf{A}) + \mathsf{WMI}(\varphi \wedge \neg\psi, w | \mathbf{X}, \mathbf{A}).
$$

Remark 3. As with remark 2, in $\mathsf{WMI}(\varphi, w | \mathbf{X}, \mathbf{A})$, specifying not only "$|\mathbf{X}$", but also "$|\mathbf{X}, \mathbf{A}$" is of primary importance. In fact, even if some of the A_m does not occur in φ,

$$
\begin{aligned}
&\mathsf{WMI}(\varphi, w | \mathbf{X}, \mathbf{A}) \\
= \ &\mathsf{WMI}(\varphi, w_{[\{A_m\}]} | \mathbf{X}, \mathbf{A} \backslash \{A_m\}) + \mathsf{WMI}(\varphi, w_{[\{\neg A_m\}]} | \mathbf{X}, \mathbf{A} \backslash \{\neg A_m\}) \\
\neq \ &\mathsf{WMI}(\varphi, w | \mathbf{X}, \mathbf{A} \backslash \{A_m\}).
\end{aligned}
$$

To this extent, hereafter and if not explicitly specified otherwise, we implicitly assume w.l.o.g. that $\mathbf{A}$ and φ are such that each Boolean atom in $\mathbf{A}$ occurs in φ. (If this were not the case, we could rewrite φ into the equivalent formula $\varphi \wedge \bigvee_k (A_k \vee \neg A_k)$, s.t. the A_k's are the atoms in $\mathbf{A}$ not occurring in φ.) Consequently, each truth assignment in $\mathcal{TTA}(\varphi)$ assigns every atom in $\mathbf{A}$. We make the same assumption w.l.o.g. for the formula $\exists \mathbf{X}.\varphi$.

The following properties of $\mathsf{WMI}(\varphi, w | \mathbf{X}, \mathbf{A})$ derive from the definition of $\mathcal{TTA}(\ldots)$.

Proposition 2. Given $\mathbf{X}$, $\mathbf{A}$, $w(\mathbf{X}, \mathbf{A})$, $\varphi(\mathbf{X}, \mathbf{A})$ and $\mathcal{TTA}(\varphi)$ as above, we have that:

$$
\mathsf{WMI}(\varphi, w | \mathbf{X}, \mathbf{A}) = \sum_{\mu^{\mathbf{A}} \wedge \mu^{\mathcal{LRA}} \in \mathcal{TTA}(\varphi)} \mathsf{WMI}_{\mathsf{nb}}(\mu^{\mathcal{LRA}}, w_{[\mu^{\mathbf{A}}]} | \mathbf{X}) \tag{4.15}
$$

Proof. By applying (4.12) to definition 5 we have that:

$$\text{WMI}(\varphi, w | \mathbf{X}, \mathbf{A}) \;\; = \;\; \sum_{\mu^{\mathbf{A}} \in \mathbb{B}^M} \;\; \sum_{\mu^{\mathcal{LRA}} \in \mathit{TTA}(\varphi_{[\mu^{\mathbf{A}}]})} \text{WMI}_{\text{nb}}(\mu^{\mathcal{LRA}}, w_{[\mu^{\mathbf{A}}]} | \mathbf{X}). \quad (4.16)$$

In order to pass from (4.16) to (4.15), consider $\mu^{\mathbf{A}} \wedge \mu^{\mathcal{LRA}}$ s.t. $\mu^{\mathbf{A}} \in \mathbb{B}^M$ and $\mu^{\mathcal{LRA}} \in \mathit{TTA}(\varphi_{[\mu^{\mathbf{A}}]})$. By construction $\mu^{\mathbf{A}} \wedge \mu^{\mathcal{LRA}} \models_{\mathbb{B}} \varphi$ (otherwise $\mu^{\mathcal{LRA}} \notin \mathit{TTA}(\varphi_{[\mu^{\mathbf{A}}]})$).
If $\mu^{\mathbf{A}} \wedge \mu^{\mathcal{LRA}} \notin \mathit{TTA}(\varphi)$, then $\mu^{\mathbf{A}} \wedge \mu^{\mathcal{LRA}}$ is not $\mathcal{LRA}$-satisfiable by the definition of $\mathit{TTA}(\varphi)$, so that $\text{WMI}_{\text{nb}}(\mu^{\mathcal{LRA}}, w_{[\mu^{\mathbf{A}}]} | \mathbf{X}) = 0$. Hence (4.16) equals (4.15). $\quad\square$

Proposition 3. Given $\mathbf{X}$, $\mathbf{A}$, $w(\mathbf{X}, \mathbf{A})$, $\varphi(\mathbf{X}, \mathbf{A})$ and $\mathit{TTA}(\varphi)$ as above, we have that:

$$\text{WMI}(\varphi, w | \mathbf{X}, \mathbf{A}) \;\; = \;\; \sum_{\mu^{\mathbf{A}} \in \mathit{TTA}(\exists \mathbf{X}. \varphi)} \text{WMI}_{\text{nb}}(\varphi_{[\mu^{\mathbf{A}}]}, w_{[\mu^{\mathbf{A}}]} | \mathbf{X}) \quad (4.17)$$

Proof. Compare (4.14) with (4.17). Let $\mu^{\mathbf{A}} \in \mathbb{B}^M$ s.t. $\mu^{\mathbf{A}} \notin \mathit{TTA}(\exists \mathbf{X}. \varphi)$. Then $\varphi_{[\mu^{\mathbf{A}}]} \Leftrightarrow_{\mathcal{LRA}} \perp$, so that $\text{WMI}_{\text{nb}}(\varphi_{[\mu^{\mathbf{A}}]}, w_{[\mu^{\mathbf{A}}]} | \mathbf{X}) = 0$. Hence (4.14) equals (4.17). $\quad\square$

Predicate abstraction in definition 3 and other forms of frequently-used formula manipulations require the introduction of fresh propositions B "labelling" sub-formulas ψ. The next result shows that this does not affect the value of WMI.

Lemma 1. Let $\mathbf{X}$, $\mathbf{A}$, w, and φ be as in definition 5; let $\psi(\mathbf{X}, \mathbf{A})$ be some $\mathcal{LRA}$-formula; let $\varphi' \overset{\text{def}}{=} \varphi \wedge (B \Longleftrightarrow \psi)$, where $B \notin \mathbf{A}$; let w' extend w s.t. $w'(\mathbf{X}, \mathbf{A} \cup \{B\}) = w(\mathbf{X}, \mathbf{A})$ for every $\mathbf{X}$, $\mathbf{A}$ and B. Then we have that

$$\text{WMI}(\varphi', w' | \mathbf{X}, \mathbf{A} \cup \{B\}) = \text{WMI}(\varphi, w | \mathbf{X}, \mathbf{A}). \quad (4.18)$$

Proof. We note that $\varphi'_{[\mu^{\mathbf{A}} \wedge B]} \Leftrightarrow_{\mathcal{LRA}} (\varphi \wedge \psi)_{[\mu^{\mathbf{A}}]}$ and that $\varphi'_{[\mu^{\mathbf{A}} \wedge \neg B]} \Leftrightarrow_{\mathcal{LRA}} (\varphi \wedge \neg\psi)_{[\mu^{\mathbf{A}}]}$. Also, we have that $w'_{[\mu^{\mathbf{A}} \wedge B]}(\mathbf{X}) = w'_{[\mu^{\mathbf{A}} \wedge \neg B]}(\mathbf{X}) = w_{[\mu^{\mathbf{A}}]}(\mathbf{X})$. Thus:

$$\text{WMI}(\varphi', w' | \mathbf{X}, \mathbf{A} \cup \{B\})$$

$$= \sum_{\mu^{\mathbf{A}} \in \mathbb{B}^M} \left(\text{WMI}_{\text{nb}}(\varphi'_{[\mu^{\mathbf{A}} \wedge B]}, w'_{[\mu^{\mathbf{A}} \wedge B]} | \mathbf{X}) + \text{WMI}_{\text{nb}}(\varphi'_{[\mu^{\mathbf{A}} \wedge \neg B]}, w'_{[\mu^{\mathbf{A}} \wedge \neg B]} | \mathbf{X}) \right)$$

$$= \sum_{\mu^{\mathbf{A}} \in \mathbb{B}^M} \left(\text{WMI}_{\text{nb}}((\varphi \wedge \psi)_{[\mu^{\mathbf{A}}]}, w_{[\mu^{\mathbf{A}}]} | \mathbf{X}) + \text{WMI}_{\text{nb}}((\varphi \wedge \neg\psi)_{[\mu^{\mathbf{A}}]}, w_{[\mu^{\mathbf{A}}]} | \mathbf{X}) \right)$$

$$= \sum_{\mu^{\mathbf{A}} \in \mathbb{B}^M} \left(\text{WMI}_{\text{nb}}(\varphi_{[\mu^{\mathbf{A}}]} \wedge \psi_{[\mu^{\mathbf{A}}]}, w_{[\mu^{\mathbf{A}}]} | \mathbf{X}) + \text{WMI}_{\text{nb}}(\varphi_{[\mu^{\mathbf{A}}]} \wedge \neg\psi_{[\mu^{\mathbf{A}}]}, w_{[\mu^{\mathbf{A}}]} | \mathbf{X}) \right)$$

$$= \sum_{\mu^{\mathbf{A}} \in \mathbb{B}^M} \text{WMI}_{\text{nb}}(\varphi_{[\mu^{\mathbf{A}}]}, w_{[\mu^{\mathbf{A}}]} | \mathbf{X})$$

$$= \text{WMI}(\varphi, w | \mathbf{X}, \mathbf{A}).$$

$\quad\square$

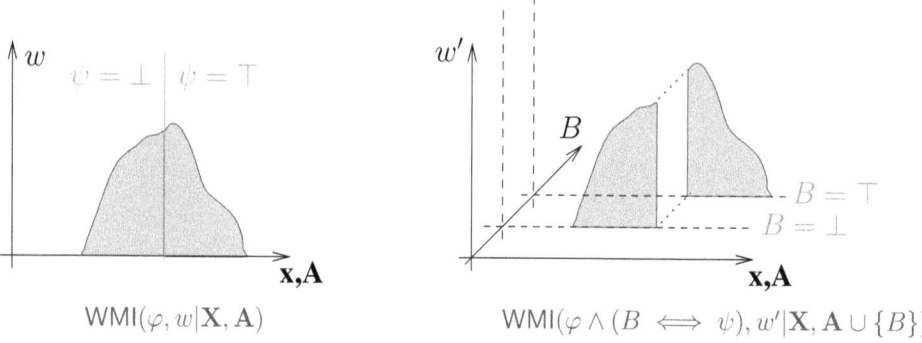

Figure 4.2: Graphical representation of Lemma 1.

The intuitive meaning of Lemma 1 is represented in Figure 4.2. (For graphical convenience, we abstract the whole space $\mathbf{X}, \mathbf{A}$ into only one horizontal dimension.) Suppose Figure 4.2 (left) represents $\mathsf{WMI}(\varphi, w|\mathbf{X}, \mathbf{A})$. The formula ψ cuts the space $\mathbf{X}, \mathbf{A}$, and thus $\mathsf{WMI}(\varphi, w|\mathbf{X}, \mathbf{A})$, into two parts. In Figure 4.2 (right) we add a new Boolean dimension B, and we represent $\mathsf{WMI}(\varphi \wedge (B \iff \psi), w'|\mathbf{X}, \mathbf{A} \cup \{B\})$, which is split into the sum of two parts, for $B = \bot$ and $B = \top$, corresponding respectively to $\psi = \bot$ and $\psi = \top$. Thus $\mathsf{WMI}(\varphi', w'|\mathbf{X}, \mathbf{A} \cup \{B\})$ is identical to the sum of the two pieces of $\mathsf{WMI}(\varphi, w|\mathbf{X}, \mathbf{A})$, for $\psi = \bot$ and $\psi = \top$ respectively.

4.2.3 Conditional Weight Functions

We call a (non-minimal) *support* of a weight function $w(\mathbf{X}, \mathbf{A})$ any subset of $\mathbb{R}^N \times \mathbb{B}^M$ out of which $w(\mathbf{X}, \mathbf{A}) = 0$. Note that a support is not unique and it is not necessarily minimal with respect to $\subseteq$, that is, it may be the case that $w(\mathbf{X}, \mathbf{A}) = 0$ also if $\langle \mathbf{X}, \mathbf{A} \rangle$ is in the support. This definition allows dealing with cases in which the minimal support is not known or hard to characterize. In many situations it is useful to provide explicitly the representation of a support of $w(\mathbf{X}, \mathbf{A})$ as a $\mathcal{LRA}$-formula $\chi(\mathbf{X}, \mathbf{A})$. (When this is not the case, then we implicitly set $\chi(\mathbf{X}, \mathbf{A}) \stackrel{\text{def}}{=} \top$.) For instance, it is useful to cut part of the domain where a polynomial function is negative.

The following property follows trivially.

Property 3. Let φ and w be as above. If $\chi(\mathbf{X}, \mathbf{A})$ is a $\mathcal{LRA}$-formula representing a support of w, then:

$$\mathsf{WMI}(\varphi, w|\mathbf{X}, \mathbf{A}) \quad = \quad \mathsf{WMI}(\varphi \wedge \chi, w|\mathbf{X}, \mathbf{A}). \tag{4.19}$$

We introduce a novel kind of weight function, which can be defined also in terms of $\mathcal{LRA}$ conditions. (See 4.3 for an example application). We consider first the generic class of functions $w(\mathbf{X})$, which we call *feasibly integrable on* $\mathcal{LRA}$ ($\mathsf{FI}^{\mathcal{LRA}}$), which contain no combinatorial component, and for which there exists some procedure able to compute $\text{WMI}_{\text{nb}}(\mu^{\mathcal{LRA}}, w|\mathbf{X})$ for every set of $\mathcal{LRA}$ literals on $\mathbf{X}$. (E.g., polynomials are $\text{FI}^{\mathcal{LRA}}$ [6]). Such background procedure, which we use as a black box, is the basic building block of our WMI calculations.

Definition 6. We call a total weight function $w(\mathbf{X}, \mathbf{A})$, **feasibly integrable under** $\mathcal{LRA}$ **conditions** ($\text{FIUC}^{\mathcal{LRA}}$) if and only if it can be described in terms of

- a support $\mathcal{LRA}$-formula $\chi(\mathbf{X}, \mathbf{A})$ (if no support description is provided, then $\chi \stackrel{\text{def}}{=} \top$),

- a set $\mathbf{\Psi} \stackrel{\text{def}}{=} \{\psi_1(\mathbf{X}, \mathbf{A}), ..., \psi_K(\mathbf{X}, \mathbf{A})\}$ of $\mathcal{LRA}$-formulas **(conditions)**,

in such a way that, for every total truth assignment $\mu^{\mathbf{A}}$ to $\mathbf{A}$ and for every total truth assignment $\mu^{\mathbf{\Psi}}$ to $\mathbf{\Psi}$, $w_{[\mu^{\mathbf{A}}\mu^{\mathbf{\Psi}}]}(\mathbf{X})$ is $\text{FI}^{\mathcal{LRA}}$ in the domain given by the values of $\langle \mathbf{X}, \mathbf{A} \rangle$ which satisfy $(\chi \wedge \mu^{\mathbf{\Psi}})_{[\mu^{\mathbf{A}}]}$. We denote such $\text{FI}^{\mathcal{LRA}}$ functions by $f_{\mu^{\mathbf{A}}\mu^{\mathbf{\Psi}}}(\mathbf{X})$, s.t. for every $\langle \mu^{\mathbf{A}}, \mu^{\mathbf{\Psi}} \rangle$,

$$\text{if } \mu^{\mathbf{A}} \wedge \mu^{\mathbf{\Psi}} \text{ holds, then } w(\mathbf{X}) = f_{\mu^{\mathbf{A}}\mu^{\mathbf{\Psi}}}(\mathbf{X}). \tag{4.20}$$

(Note that a plain $\text{FI}^{\mathcal{LRA}}$ weight function is a subcase in which $\chi \stackrel{\text{def}}{=} \top$ and $\mathbf{\Psi} \stackrel{\text{def}}{=} \varnothing$.)

A very relevant subcase of $\text{FIUC}^{\mathcal{LRA}}$ functions, which we denote by $\text{P}^{\mathcal{LRA}}$ ("Polynomials under $\mathcal{LRA}$ conditions"), is given by arbitrary combinations of polynomials with $\mathcal{LRA}$ conditions, such that each $f_{\mu^{\mathbf{A}}\mu^{\mathbf{\Psi}}}(\mathbf{X})$ in (4.20) is a polynomial whose value is non-negative in the domain defined by $\mu^{\mathbf{\Psi}}$. $\text{P}^{\mathcal{LRA}}$ functions are $\text{FIUC}^{\mathcal{LRA}}$ because polynomials can always be integrated on the domains given by a set of $\mathcal{LRA}$ literals [6]. The syntax of $\text{P}^{\mathcal{LRA}}$ weight functions can be defined by the following grammar, expressed in standard Backus-Naur form: [2]

$$
\begin{aligned}
w \quad ::= \quad & c \mid x \mid \tag{4.21}\\
& -w \mid (w+w) \mid (w-w) \mid (w \cdot w) \mid \\
& [\![\text{If } \varphi \text{ Then } w \text{ Else } w]\!] \mid \\
& [\![\text{Case } \varphi : w; \varphi : w; ...]\!] \\
\chi \quad ::= \quad & \varphi \tag{4.22}
\end{aligned}
$$

where c denotes a real value, x denotes a real variable, w denotes a $\text{P}^{\mathcal{LRA}}$ weight function, φ denotes an $\mathcal{LRA}$ formula. We stress that the conditions φ in the case-terms must be mutually exclusive and exhaustive. (In practice, it suffices that the conditions are exhaustive *within the domain described by the support* χ, that is, for the term $[\![\text{Case } \varphi_1 : w_1; \varphi_2 : w_2; ... \varphi_k : w_k]\!]$ we must have that $\chi \models_{\mathcal{LRA}} \bigvee_{i=1}^{k} \varphi_i$.) In short, w can be any arbitrary combination of sums, products and $\mathcal{LRA}$-conditions.

Note that all the $\mathcal{LRA}$-formulas φ occurring as conditions in the weight function or in the support formula must be such to restrict the domains of the polynomials to areas where they are non-negative.

---

[2]The obvious standard syntactic simplifications apply, e.g., "$((1 \cdot x_1) - (4 \cdot x_2)) + -(5 \cdot x_3))$" is rewritten as "$(x_1 - 4x_2 - 5x_3)$".

Example 15. Let $\mathbf{X} \overset{\text{def}}{=} \{x_1, x_2\}$, $\mathbf{A} \overset{\text{def}}{=} \{A\}$, and

$$\chi(\mathbf{X}, \mathbf{A}) \overset{\text{def}}{=} [\![x_1 \in [-1, 1)]\!] \wedge [\![x_2 \in [-1, 1)]\!] \wedge (A \iff (x_2 \geq 0))$$

$$w(\mathbf{X}, \mathbf{A}) \overset{\text{def}}{=} [\![\text{If } x_1 \geq 0 \text{ Then } x_1^3 \text{ Else } - 2x_1]\!] + [\![\text{If } A \text{ Then } 3x_2 \text{ Else } - x_2^5]\!].$$

w is $\mathsf{P}^{\mathcal{LRA}}$, and hence $\mathsf{FIUC}^{\mathcal{LRA}}$. In fact, its value depends on the combination of the truth values of the conditions $\boldsymbol{\Psi} \overset{\text{def}}{=} \{(x_1 \geq 0)\}$ and $\mathbf{A} \overset{\text{def}}{=} \{A\}$, so that:

$$\begin{aligned}
f_{\{A,(x_1 \geq 0)\}} &= x_1^3 + 3x_2 & \text{s.t. } x_1 \in [0, 1),\ x_2 \in [0, 1), \\
f_{\{A,\neg(x_1 \geq 0)\}} &= -2x_1 + 3x_2, & \text{s.t. } x_1 \in [-1, 0),\ x_2 \in [0, 1), \\
f_{\{\neg A,(x_1 \geq 0)\}} &= x_1^3 - x_2^5, & \text{s.t. } x_1 \in [0, 1),\ x_2 \in [-1, 0), \\
f_{\{\neg A,\neg(x_1 \geq 0)\}} &= -2x_1 - x_2^5 & \text{s.t. } x_1 \in [-1, 0),\ x_2 \in [-1, 0).
\end{aligned}$$

All four $f_{\mu^{\mathbf{A}}\mu^{\boldsymbol{\Psi}}}$ are positive polynomials in their respective domain and as such they can be integrated.

Intuitively, definition 6 captures the class of all the weight functions which can be described by means of arbitrary combinations of nested if-then-elses on conditions in $\mathbf{A}$ and $\boldsymbol{\Psi}$, s.t. each branch $\langle \mu^{\mathbf{A}}, \mu^{\boldsymbol{\Psi}} \rangle$ results into a $\mathsf{FI}^{\mathcal{LRA}}$ weight function. Each pair $\langle \mu^{\mathbf{A}}, \mu^{\boldsymbol{\Psi}} \rangle$ describes a portion of the domain of w, inside which w is the $\mathsf{FI}^{\mathcal{LRA}}$ function $f_{\mu^{\mathbf{A}}\mu^{\boldsymbol{\Psi}}}$.

The expressivity of $\mathsf{FIUC}^{\mathcal{LRA}}$ weight functions allows the direct encoding of a number of probabilistic models or density estimators into the weighted model integration framework. For instance, it is possible to readily perform WMI inference on a trained *Mixed Sum-Product Network* (MSPN) [72] with piecewise-polynomial leaves, whose internal nodes are product or weighted sums. In this case, the circuit is already a $\mathsf{FIUC}^{\mathcal{LRA}}$ function and the support corresponds to the disjunction of the domains of its polynomial leaves. This procedure allows MSPNs to answer complex probability queries that couldn't normally be computed by their inference algorithms, such as those involving hard constraints. *Density Estimation Trees* (DETs) [86] are hybrid density estimators composed of internal univariate split nodes and constant leaves. Also in this case, the tree can be represented by a $\mathsf{FIUC}^{\mathcal{LRA}}$ function without additional processing and probabilistic queries can be performed using the estimator's bounding box as the support, thus enabling probabilistic queries on DETs.

Theorem 1. Let $w(\mathbf{X}, \mathbf{A})$, $\boldsymbol{\Psi}$ and χ be as in definition 6. Let $\mathbf{B} \overset{\text{def}}{=} \{B_1, ..., B_K\}$ be fresh propositional atoms and let $w^*(\mathbf{X}, \mathbf{A} \cup \mathbf{B})$ be the weight function obtained by substituting in $w(\mathbf{X}, \mathbf{A})$ each condition ψ_k with B_k, for every $k \in [1..K]$. Let

$$\varphi^* \overset{\text{def}}{=} \varphi \wedge \chi \wedge \bigwedge_{k=1}^{K} (B_k \iff \psi_k)$$

Then:

$$\mathsf{WMI}(\varphi \wedge \chi, w | \mathbf{X}, \mathbf{A}) = \mathsf{WMI}(\varphi^*, w^* | \mathbf{X}, \mathbf{A} \cup \mathbf{B}). \tag{4.23}$$

Proof. To every truth assignment $\mu^{\boldsymbol{\Psi}}$ to $\boldsymbol{\Psi}$ we associate the corresponding truth assignment

$\mu^{\mathbf{B}}$ to $\mathbf{B}$ s.t. $\mu^{\mathbf{B}}(B_k) = \mu^{\mathbf{\Psi}}(\psi_k)$, for every $k \in [1..K]$. We note that, for every $\mu^{\mathbf{A}} \in \mathbb{B}^M$ and $\mu^{\mathbf{B}} \in \mathbb{B}^K$ (with its corresponding $\mu^{\mathbf{\Psi}}$):

$$\varphi^*_{[\mu^{\mathbf{A}} \wedge \mu^{\mathbf{B}}]} \Leftrightarrow_{\mathcal{LRA}} (\varphi \wedge \chi \wedge \mu^{\mathbf{\Psi}})_{[\mu^{\mathbf{A}} \wedge \mu^{\mathbf{B}}]}, \tag{4.24}$$

because every ψ_k is forced by $\mu^{\mathbf{\Psi}}$ to assume the same truth value B_k assumes in $\mu^{\mathbf{B}}$. Let w' extend w s.t. $w'(\mathbf{X}, \mathbf{A} \cup \mathbf{B}) = w(\mathbf{X}, \mathbf{A})$ for every $\mathbf{X}$, $\mathbf{A}$ and $\mathbf{B}$. Then, since φ^* forces every B_k to hold if and only if Ψ_k holds, we have:

$$\mathsf{WMI}_{\mathsf{nb}}(\varphi^*_{[\mu^{\mathbf{A}} \wedge \mu^{\mathbf{B}}]}, w'_{[\mu^{\mathbf{A}} \wedge \mu^{\mathbf{B}}]} | \mathbf{X}) \tag{4.25}$$

$$= \mathsf{WMI}_{\mathsf{nb}}((\varphi \wedge \chi \wedge \mu^{\mathbf{\Psi}})_{[\mu^{\mathbf{A}} \wedge \mu^{\mathbf{B}}]}, w'_{[\mu^{\mathbf{A}} \wedge \mu^{\mathbf{B}}]} | \mathbf{X})$$

$$= \mathsf{WMI}_{\mathsf{nb}}((\varphi \wedge \chi \wedge \mu^{\mathbf{\Psi}})_{[\mu^{\mathbf{A}} \wedge \mu^{\mathbf{B}}]}, f_{\mu^{\mathbf{A}} \mu^{\mathbf{\Psi}}} | \mathbf{X})$$

$$= \mathsf{WMI}_{\mathsf{nb}}((\varphi \wedge \chi \wedge \mu^{\mathbf{\Psi}})_{[\mu^{\mathbf{A}} \wedge \mu^{\mathbf{B}}]}, w^*_{[\mu^{\mathbf{A}} \wedge \mu^{\mathbf{B}}]} | \mathbf{X})$$

$$= \mathsf{WMI}_{\mathsf{nb}}(\varphi^*_{[\mu^{\mathbf{A}} \wedge \mu^{\mathbf{B}}]}, w^*_{[\mu^{\mathbf{A}} \wedge \mu^{\mathbf{B}}]} | \mathbf{X}).$$

Then, by applying K times Lemma 1, and then (4.25):

$$\mathsf{WMI}(\varphi \wedge \chi, w | \mathbf{X}, \mathbf{A})$$

$$= \mathsf{WMI}(\varphi \wedge \chi \wedge \bigwedge_{k=1}^{K} (B_k \iff \psi_k), w' | \mathbf{X}, \mathbf{A} \cup \mathbf{B})$$

$$= \sum_{\mu^{\mathbf{A}} \in \mathbb{B}^M \mu^{\mathbf{B}} \in \mathbb{B}^K} \mathsf{WMI}_{\mathsf{nb}}(\varphi^*_{[\mu^{\mathbf{A}} \wedge \mu^{\mathbf{B}}]}, w'_{[\mu^{\mathbf{A}} \wedge \mu^{\mathbf{B}}]} | \mathbf{X})$$

$$= \sum_{\mu^{\mathbf{A}} \in \mathbb{B}^M \mu^{\mathbf{B}} \in \mathbb{B}^K} \mathsf{WMI}_{\mathsf{nb}}(\varphi^*_{[\mu^{\mathbf{A}} \wedge \mu^{\mathbf{B}}]}, w^*_{[\mu^{\mathbf{A}} \wedge \mu^{\mathbf{B}}]} | \mathbf{X})$$

$$= \mathsf{WMI}(\varphi^*, w^* | \mathbf{X}, \mathbf{A} \cup \mathbf{B}).$$

$\square$

Example 16. Consider the case with no propositional variables $\mathbf{A} = \varnothing$:

$$\chi \overset{\text{def}}{=} [\![x \in [-1, 1]]\!]$$

$$\varphi \overset{\text{def}}{=} \top$$

$$\psi \overset{\text{def}}{=} (x \geq 0)$$

$$w(x) \overset{\text{def}}{=} [\![\mathsf{If}\ (x \geq 0)\ \mathsf{Then}\ x\ \mathsf{Else} - x]\!] = |x|$$

Then

$$\mathsf{WMI}(\varphi, w | \{x\}, \varnothing) = \mathsf{WMI}_{\mathsf{nb}}(\varphi, w | \mathbf{X}) = \int_{[-1,1]} |x| dx = 1$$

By Lemma 1, $\varphi^* = [\![x \in [-1, 1]]\!] \wedge (B \iff (x \geq 0))$ and $w^* = [\![\mathsf{If}\ B\ \mathsf{Then}\ x\ \mathsf{Else} - x]\!]$, which are the same formula and weight function as in Example 14 (modulo some reordering and variable renaming), s.t. $\mathsf{WMI}(\varphi^*, w^* | \mathbf{X}, \mathbf{B}) = 1$

Theorem 1 enables the computation of WMI with complicated FIUC$^{\mathcal{LRA}}$ weight functions by substituting with a fresh Boolean variable B_k each condition ψ_k in the if-then-else and case constructs and by adding $\bigwedge_{k=1}^{K}(B_k \iff \psi_k)$ to $\varphi \wedge \chi$. Intuitively, during the computation of the WMIs, Theorem 1 allows extracting out of the integrals the conditional component on $\mathcal{LRA}$ conditions, which are labeled by Boolean atoms and can be thus handled externally. Note that the pairs of truth assignments $\langle \mu^{\mathbf{A}}, \mu^{\mathbf{\Psi}} \rangle$ of practical interest are only those for which $(\chi \wedge \mu^{\mathbf{\Psi}})_{[\mu^{\mathbf{A}}]}$ is $\mathcal{LRA}$-satisfiable. We will address this issue in 4.4.

4.2.4   From WMI to WMI$_{\mathrm{old}}$ and vice versa

We can now compare the original definition of WMI in [10] (definition of WMI$_{\mathrm{old}}$ in 2.3) with our new notion of WMI applied to FIUC$^{\mathcal{LRA}}$ weight functions. One key difference is that in the former the weight w is defined as a *product of weights on literals in* φ, whereas with the latter the weight w is a FIUC$^{\mathcal{LRA}}$ function over the $\mathcal{LRA}$ domain $\langle \mathbf{X}, \mathbf{A} \rangle$ (and hence it does not depend on the $\mathcal{LRA}$-atoms in φ).

To this extent, we note that we can easily express and compute WMI$_{\mathrm{old}}$ (2.3) as WMI in the following way, by using an equivalent FIUC$^{\mathcal{LRA}}$ weight function:

$$\mathsf{WMI}(\varphi, \prod_{\psi \in Atoms(\varphi)} [\![\text{If } \psi \text{ Then } w(\psi) \text{ Else } w(\neg\psi)]\!] | \mathbf{X}, \mathbf{A}).$$

The vice versa is tricky, in the sense that, to the best of our knowledge and understanding, there is no obvious general way to encode an arbitrary FIUC$^{\mathcal{LRA}}$ weight function into a WMI$_{\mathrm{old}}$ one while always preventing an explosion in the size of its representation. In order to understand the difficulty in finding such a general encoding, consider a *generic* FIUC$^{\mathcal{LRA}}$ weight function $w(\mathbf{X}, \mathbf{A})$. In order to write it as a WMI$_{\mathrm{old}}$ weight function, one should find an integer K, a set of conditions $\{\psi_k(\mathbf{X}, \mathbf{A})\}_{k=1}^{K}$ and a set of positive functions $\{f_{\psi_k}(\mathbf{X}), f_{\neg\psi_k}(\mathbf{X})\}_{k=1}^{K}$ so that $w(\mathbf{X}, \mathbf{A})$ could be written into the WMI$_{\mathrm{old}}$-equivalent form:

$$w(\mathbf{X}, \mathbf{A}) \quad = \quad \prod_{k=1}^{K} [\![\text{If } \psi_k(\mathbf{X}, \mathbf{A}) \text{ Then } f_{\psi_k}(\mathbf{X}) \text{ Else } f_{\neg\psi_k}(\mathbf{X})]\!] \tag{4.26}$$

where the conditions ψ_k can be either (a) Boolean atoms in $\mathbf{A}$, (b) $\mathcal{LRA}$-atoms on $\mathbf{X}$, (c) $\mathcal{LRA}$-formulas on atoms in the form (a) and (b) by labeling them with fresh Boolean atoms, so that their truth values derive deterministically from the values of $\mathbf{X}, \mathbf{A}$, written "$\psi_k(\mathbf{X}, \mathbf{A})$".

Since $w(\mathbf{X}, \mathbf{A})$, $f_{\psi_k}(\mathbf{X})$ and $f_{\neg\psi_k}(\mathbf{X})$ are positive for every k, and the *log* function is continuous, strictly increasing and invertible, noticing that:

$$[\![\text{If } A \text{ Then } b \text{ Else } c]\!] = [\![\text{If } A \text{ Then } b \text{ Else } 0]\!] + [\![\text{If } A \text{ Then } 0 \text{ Else } c]\!]$$

we see that (4.26) is equivalent to:

$$log(w(\mathbf{X}, \mathbf{A})) \quad = \quad \sum_{k=1}^{K} \begin{array}{l} [\![\text{If } \psi_k(\mathbf{X}, \mathbf{A}) \text{ Then } log(f_{\psi_k}(\mathbf{X})) \text{ Else } 0]\!] + \\ [\![\text{If } \psi_k(\mathbf{X}, \mathbf{A}) \text{ Then } 0 \text{ Else } log(f_{\neg\psi_k}(\mathbf{X}))]\!] \end{array} \quad (4.27)$$

for every $\mathbf{X}, \mathbf{A}$. Thus, if we fix the value for $\mathbf{X}$ and call $y_{k\top} \overset{\text{def}}{=} log(f_{\psi_k}(\mathbf{X}))$ and $y_{k\perp} \overset{\text{def}}{=}$ $log(f_{\neg\psi_k}(\mathbf{X}))$ s.t. $y_{k\top}, y_{k\perp} \in \mathbb{R} \cup \{-\infty\}$, then (4.27) can be represented as a system of $2^{|\mathbf{A}|}$ linear equalities, one for each total truth assignment on $\mathbf{A}$, on $2K$ variables $\{y_{k\top}, y_{k\perp}\}_{k=1}^{K}$ whose $\{0, 1\}$-coefficients are given by the truth values of $\psi_k(\mathbf{X}, \mathbf{A})$. Thus, for every value of $\mathbf{X}$, we have $2^{|\mathbf{A}|}$ linear equations with $2K$ real-valued variables. This suggests that, in order (4.26) to hold, the size K of the product may blow up in size with $|\mathbf{A}|$.

For instance, a trivial general solution consists in first converting the problem into $\mathsf{WMI}(\varphi^*, w^*|\mathbf{X}, \mathbf{A}^*)$ as in Theorem 1 and then, *for every total truth assignment μ in $TTA(\varphi^*)$*, introducing a fresh new Boolean atom B_μ adding $B_\mu \iff \mu$ to the formula, and defining $w(B_\mu) \overset{\text{def}}{=} w_\mu(\mathbf{X})$, $w(\neg B_\mu) \overset{\text{def}}{=} 1$, $w(l) \overset{\text{def}}{=} 1$ for every other literal l. This solution is obviously not practical for non-trivial size of $\mathbf{A}^*$ because it generates an exponential growth in the size of the formula.

4.3   A Case Study

Consider modelling journey time on a road network for e.g. a delivery agency. In order to safely organize priority deliveries, the agency could be interested in knowing well in advance the probability of completing the journey within a certain time, given the time of departure. An accurate estimate requires to consider how travel duration between locations can change according to the time of the day, and combine these duration distributions over the entire route. A different encoding for the same problem was presented in the original WMI work [10].

Suppose that (the part of interest of) the day is partitioned into $\{I^1, ..., I^M\}$ disjoint and consecutive intervals such that, for each adjacent location l_i and l_j in the road network and for each $I^m \overset{\text{def}}{=} [c_m, c_{m+1})$, we know the distribution of the journey time from location l_i to location l_j given that we move at time $t \in I^m$. Let $f_{l_i, l_j}^m : \mathbb{R} \mapsto \mathbb{R}^+$ denote such distribution and let the interval $R_{l_i, l_j}^m \overset{\text{def}}{=} [a_{l_i, l_j}^m, b_{l_i, l_j}^m)$ be its support. (Note that the I^ms are intervals in absolute time and are all disjoint whereas the R_{l_i, l_j}^ms are intervals in relative time and are typically not disjoint.)

4.3.1   Modelling a journey with a fixed path

Given a path $(l_0, ..., l_N)$ and departure and arrival times t_{dep} and t_{arr}, we are interested in answering queries of the form

$$P(t_N \leq t_{\mathsf{arr}} \mid t_0 = t_{\mathsf{dep}}, \{l_i\}_{i=0}^{N})$$

We can encode the problem as follows. Let t_n be the time at step n and x_n the journey time between l_{n-1} and l_n. Let $\mathbf{X} \stackrel{\text{def}}{=} \{x_1, ..., x_N\}$. (Here $\mathbf{A} \stackrel{\text{def}}{=} \varnothing$.) Then:

$$\chi(\mathbf{X}) \stackrel{\text{def}}{=} \bigwedge_{n=0}^{N} [\![t_n \in [c_1, c_{M+1}]]\!] \wedge \bigwedge_{n=1}^{N} [\![\text{OneOf}\{[\![t_{n-1} \in I^m]\!]\}_{m=1}^{M}]\!]$$

$$\wedge \bigwedge_{n=1}^{N} \bigwedge_{m=1}^{M} ([\![t_{n-1} \in I^m]\!] \rightarrow [\![x_n \in R^m_{l_{n-1}, l_n}]\!])$$

$$w(\mathbf{X}) \stackrel{\text{def}}{=} \prod_{n=1}^{N} \left[\text{Case } [\![t_{n-1} \in I^1]\!] : f^1_{l_{n-1}, l_n}(x_n); \ ... \ [\![t_{n-1} \in I^M]\!] : f^M_{l_{n-1}, l_n}(x_n) \right]$$

$$\varphi(\mathbf{X}) \stackrel{\text{def}}{=} \top,$$

where for $n > 0$, "t_n" is a shortcut for the term "$\sum_{i=1}^{n} x_i + t_0$", so that "$[\![t_{n-1} \in I^m]\!]$" is a shortcut for the formula "$(\sum_{i=1}^{n-1} x_i + t_0 \geq c_m) \wedge \neg (\sum_{i=1}^{n-1} x_i + t_0 \geq c_{m+1})$", and "$[\![x_n \in R^m_{l_{n-1}, l_n}]\!]$" is a shortcut for the formula "$(x_n \geq a^m_{l_{n-1}, l_n}) \wedge \neg (x_n \geq b^m_{l_{n-1}, l_n})$".

This encoding allows us to answer the up-mentioned queries as follows:

$$P(t_N \leq t_{\text{arr}} \mid t_0 = t_{\text{dep}}, \{l_i\}_{i=0}^{N}) = \frac{\text{WMI}_{\text{nb}}(\chi(\mathbf{X}) \wedge (t_N \leq t_{\text{arr}}) \wedge (t_0 = t_{\text{dep}}), w(\mathbf{X}) \mid \mathbf{X})}{\text{WMI}_{\text{nb}}(\chi(\mathbf{X}) \wedge (t_0 = t_{\text{dep}}), w(\mathbf{X}) \mid \mathbf{X})}$$

where the locations $\{l_i\}_{i=0}^{N}$ are used to generate a query-specific encoding for $\chi(\mathbf{X})$ and $w(\mathbf{X})$.

Under the assumption that each distribution $f^m_{l_i, l_j}(x)$ is feasibly integrable if $x \in R^m_{l_i, l_j}$, then $w(\mathbf{X})$ is $\text{FIUC}^{\mathcal{LRA}}$ with $N \cdot M$ conditions $\psi^m_n \stackrel{\text{def}}{=} [\![t_n \in I^m]\!]$. Thus we can introduce $N \cdot M$ fresh Boolean atoms B^m_n and apply Theorem 1, obtaining:

$$\varphi^*(\mathbf{X}, \mathbf{B}) \stackrel{\text{def}}{=} \varphi(\mathbf{X}) \wedge \chi(\mathbf{X}) \wedge \bigwedge_{n=1}^{N} \bigwedge_{m=1}^{M} (B^m_{n-1} \iff [\![t_{n-1} \in I^m]\!])$$

$$w^*(\mathbf{X}, \mathbf{B}) \stackrel{\text{def}}{=} \prod_{n=1}^{N} \left[\text{Case } B^1_{n-1} : f^1_{l_{n-1}, l_n}(x_n); \ ... \ B^M_{n-1} : f^M_{l_{n-1}, l_n}(x_n) \right].$$

Each distribution $f^m_{l_{n-1}, l_n}$ is thus associated to B^m_n. Note that, for each step n, exactly one condition variable B^m_n is true, representing the fact that the n-th location is reached during the m-th interval. Intuitively, this allows the algorithm to select at each step the distribution corresponding to the interval in which the location is reached, as shown in Figure 4.3.

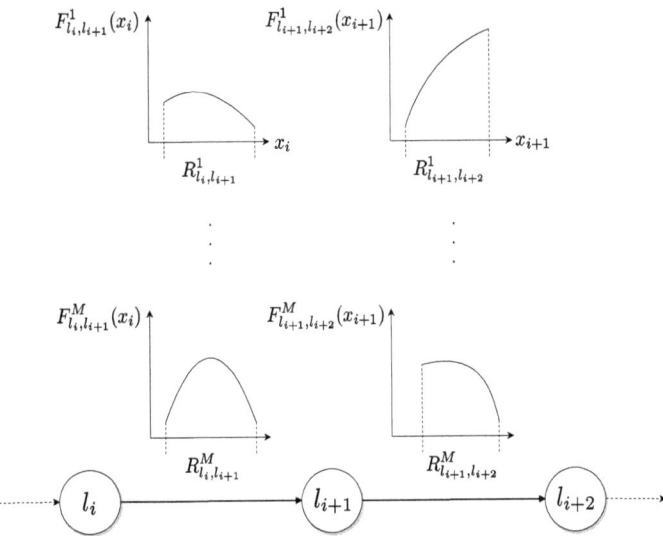

Figure 4.3: This figure shows the journey time densities for a pair of consecutive time steps, from location l_i to l_{i+2}. Each edge shows the corresponding journey time distribution for each of the intervals.

Example 17. Consider an instance of our case study where $\mathbf{A} \overset{\text{def}}{=} \varnothing$, $N = 2$, $M = 3$,

$$\chi(\mathbf{X}) \overset{\text{def}}{=} [\![t_0 \in [7, 10)]\!]$$
$$\wedge [\![t_0 + x_1 \in [7, 10)]\!]$$
$$\wedge [\![\mathsf{OneOf}\{[\![t_0 \in [7, 8)]\!], ..., [\![t_0 \in [9, 10)]\!]\}]\!]$$
$$\wedge [\![\mathsf{OneOf}\{[\![t_0 + x_1 \in [7, 8)]\!], ..., [\![t_0 + x_1 \in [9, 10)]\!]\}]\!]$$
$$\wedge [\![t_0 \in [7, 8)]\!] \rightarrow [\![x_1 \in [0.5, 1)]\!]$$
$$\wedge [\![t_0 \in [8, 9)]\!] \rightarrow [\![x_1 \in [1, 1.5)]\!]$$
$$\wedge [\![t_0 \in [9, 10)]\!] \rightarrow [\![x_1 \in [1, 2)]\!]$$
$$\wedge [\![t_0 + x_1 \in [7, 8)]\!] \rightarrow [\![x_2 \in [1, 1.5)]\!]$$
$$\wedge [\![t_0 + x_1 \in [8, 9)]\!] \rightarrow [\![x_2 \in [1.5, 2)]\!]$$
$$\wedge [\![t_0 + x_1 \in [9, 10)]\!] \rightarrow [\![x_2 \in [1, 2)]\!]$$

$$w(\mathbf{X}) \overset{\text{def}}{=} \begin{bmatrix} \mathsf{Case} & \\ [\![t_0 \in [7, 8)]\!] & : f_{l_0 l_1}^1(x_1); \\ [\![t_0 \in [8, 9)]\!] & : f_{l_0 l_1}^2(x_1); \\ [\![t_0 \in [9, 10)]\!] & : f_{l_0 l_1}^3(x_1); \end{bmatrix} \cdot \begin{bmatrix} \mathsf{Case} & \\ [\![t_0 + x_1 \in [7, 8)]\!] & : f_{l_1 l_2}^1(x_2); \\ [\![t_0 + x_1 \in [8, 9)]\!] & : f_{l_1 l_2}^2(x_2); \\ [\![t_0 + x_1 \in [9, 10)]\!] & : f_{l_1 l_2}^3(x_2); \end{bmatrix}$$

$$\varphi(\mathbf{X}) \overset{\text{def}}{=} \top$$

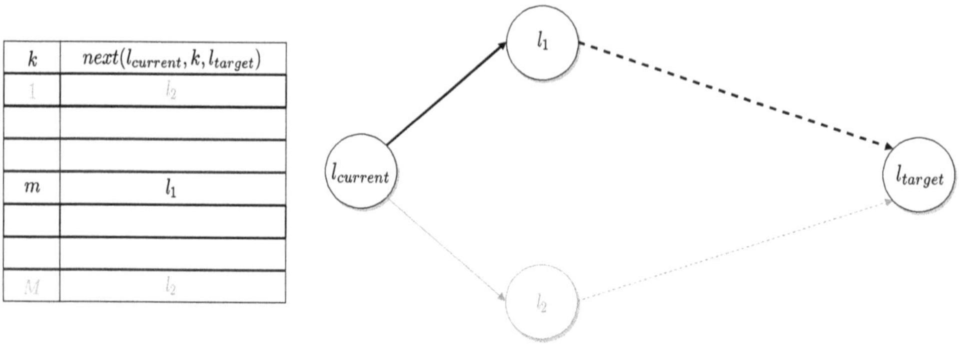

Figure 4.4: The figure shows two alternative (sub)paths from l_{curr} to l_{target}: the successor of l_{curr} is selected according to the time interval at which the node is reached (m in the figure).

where the $f^m_{l_{n-1}l_n}(x_n)$ are functions which are integrable and positive in their respective domain stated in $\chi(\mathbf{X})$ (e.g., $f^1_{l_0 l_1}(x_1)$ is integrable and positive in $[\![x_1 \in [0.5, 1)]\!]$).

Then, by applying Theorem 1, we can introduce 6 Boolean variables B^m_n and reformulate the problem as follows:

$$\begin{aligned}\varphi^*(\mathbf{X}, \mathbf{B}) &\stackrel{\text{def}}{=} \varphi(\mathbf{X}) \wedge \chi(\mathbf{X}) \\ &\wedge \ (B^1_0 \iff [\![t_0 \in [7, 8)]\!]) \\ &\wedge \ \ldots \\ &\wedge \ (B^3_1 \iff [\![t_0 + x_1 \in [9, 10)]\!])\end{aligned} \tag{4.28}$$

$$w^*(\mathbf{X}, \mathbf{B}) \stackrel{\text{def}}{=} \left[\!\!\left[\begin{array}{ll}\mathsf{Case} & \\ B^1_0 & : f^1_{l_0 l_1}(x_1); \\ B^2_0 & : f^2_{l_0 l_1}(x_1); \\ B^3_0 & : f^3_{l_0 l_1}(x_1);\end{array}\right]\!\!\right] \cdot \left[\!\!\left[\begin{array}{ll}\mathsf{Case} & \\ B^1_1 & : f^1_{l_1 l_2}(x_2); \\ B^2_1 & : f^2_{l_1 l_2}(x_2); \\ B^3_1 & : f^3_{l_1 l_2}(x_2);\end{array}\right]\!\!\right]$$

4.3.2 Modelling a journey under a conditional plan

We generalize the previous scenario to the case in which the path is not given in advance. Rather, they are provided only a maximum path length N, a final target location l_{target} and a *conditional plan*, establishing the successor location for every location at each time slot. Intuitively, the conditional plan mimics the empirical knowledge of a driver that, given his/her current location and time of the day, chooses the next step towards the final destination. (E.g., if one road passes aside a school entrance, the driver arriving there from 8am to 9am knows it is better to choose an alternative path to avoid the queues of cars leaving the children there.)

Let $\mathcal{I} = \{1, ..., M\}$ be the set of indices of the time intervals. Let $\mathcal{L} = \{1, ..., L\}$ be the set of indices of each location. Given a target destination $l_{\mathsf{target}} \in \mathcal{L}$, a *conditional plan* is a function $\mathsf{next} : \mathcal{L} \times \mathcal{I} \times \mathcal{L} \to \mathcal{L}$ such that, for any current location $l \in \mathcal{L}$ and time interval index $m \in \mathcal{I}$,

$\text{next}(l, m, l_{\text{target}})$ is the next location in the path, as shown in Figure 4.4. To handle the special case of the final location l_{target}, we set $\text{next}(l_{\text{target}}, m, l_{\text{target}}) \stackrel{\text{def}}{=} l_{\text{target}}$ and $R^m_{l_{\text{target}}, l_{\text{target}}} \stackrel{\text{def}}{=} [0, 0]$, so that $[\![x \in R^m_{l_{\text{target}}, l_{\text{target}}}]\!] \stackrel{\text{def}}{=} (x = 0)$. The queries we want to address are of the form:

$$P(t_N \leq t_{\text{arr}} \mid t_0 = t_{\text{dep}}, l_{\text{dep}}, l_{\text{target}}, \text{next}).$$

The encoding generalizes the previous encoding for fixed paths. This time we need to introduce N sets of L mutually-exclusive Boolean variables $A_{n,l}$ which encode the location visited at each time step – with the intended meaning that $A_{n,l}$ is true if and only if the location at step n is the one indexed by l – and $[\![\text{OneOf}\{A_{n,l} \mid l \in [1, L]\}]\!]$ is added to the formula for every n. When L is large enough, this can be alternatively encoded by a distinct truth assignment to $\lceil log_2(L) \rceil$ Boolean variables representing the binary encoding of the index l, using overall $N \cdot \lceil log_2(L) \rceil$ Boolean variables. Unless otherwise specified, in the following we use the same notation and shortcuts of the case study presented in 4.3 (in particular, we recall that for $n > 0$, "t_n" is a shortcut for the term "$\sum_{i=1}^{n} x_i + t_0$"):

$$\chi(\mathbf{X}, \mathbf{A}) \stackrel{\text{def}}{=} \bigwedge_{n=0}^{N} [\![t_n \in [c_1, c_{M+1}]]\!] \wedge \bigwedge_{n=1}^{N} [\![\text{OneOf}\{[\![t_{n-1} \in I^m]\!] \mid m \in [1, M]\}]\!]$$

$$\wedge \bigwedge_{n=0}^{N} [\![\text{OneOf}\{A_{n,l} \mid l \in [1, L]\}]\!]$$

$$\wedge \bigwedge_{n=1}^{N} \left(\bigwedge_{l=1}^{L} \left(A_{n-1,l} \to \bigwedge_{m=1}^{M} ([\![t_{n-1} \in I^m]\!] \to [\![x_n \in R^m_{l,\text{next}(l,m,l_{\text{target}})}]\!]) \right) \right),$$

$$\varphi(\mathbf{X}, \mathbf{A}) \stackrel{\text{def}}{=} A_{0, l_0} \wedge \bigwedge_{n=1}^{N} \left(\bigwedge_{l=1}^{L} \left(A_{n-1,l} \to \bigwedge_{m=1}^{M} ([\![t_{n-1} \in I^m]\!] \to A_{n, \text{next}(l,m,l_{\text{target}})}) \right) \right)$$

$$w(\mathbf{X}, \mathbf{A}) \stackrel{\text{def}}{=} \prod_{n=1}^{N} \begin{bmatrix} \text{Case} \\ (A_{n-1,l_1} \wedge A_{n,l_2}) : \\ \quad [\![\text{Case } [\![t_{n-1} \in I^1]\!] : f^1_{l_1,l_2}(x_n); \dots ; [\![t_{n-1} \in I^M]\!] : f^M_{l_1,l_2}(x_n)]\!]; \\ (A_{n-1,l_1} \wedge A_{n,l_3}) : \\ \quad [\![\text{Case } [\![t_{n-1} \in I^1]\!] : f^1_{l_1,l_3}(x_n); \dots ; [\![t_{n-1} \in I^M]\!] : f^M_{l_1,l_3}(x_n)]\!]; \\ \dots \\ (A_{n-1,l_L} \wedge A_{n,l_{L-1}}) : \\ \quad [\![\text{Case } [\![t_{n-1} \in I^1]\!] : f^1_{l_L,l_{L-1}}(x_n); \dots ; [\![t_{n-1} \in I^M]\!] : f^M_{l_L,l_{L-1}}(x_n)]\!]; \end{bmatrix}$$

Note that in the definition of $w(\mathbf{X}, \mathbf{A})$ the pairs of locations of interest in the outer case-expression are only those connected by an edge. Moreover, we can safely consider only the edges which appear in the conditional plan for the desired l_{target}, i.e. pairs in

$$\mathcal{L}_{\text{reach}} = \{\langle l_i, l_j \rangle \mid l_i \neq l_j \in \mathcal{L}, \exists m \in [1, M] . \text{next}(l_i, m, l_{\text{target}}) = l_j\}.$$

If we compare the description of $\chi(\mathbf{X})$, $w(\mathbf{X})$ and $\varphi(\mathbf{X})$ for the fixed-path-setting in 4.3.1 with these of $\chi(\mathbf{X}, \mathbf{A})$, $w(\mathbf{X}, \mathbf{A})$ and $\varphi(\mathbf{X}, \mathbf{A})$ for the conditional-plan setting described above, we note that the former can be seen as a particular subcase of the latter. In fact, if we impose a given path $l_0, l_1, ..., l_N$ by substituting the part "$A_{0,l_0} \wedge \bigwedge_{n=1}^{N}(...)$" in $\varphi(\mathbf{X}, \mathbf{A})$ with "$\bigwedge_{n=0}^{N} A_{n,l_n}$", then it is easy to see that $\chi(\mathbf{X}, \mathbf{A}) \wedge \varphi(\mathbf{X}, \mathbf{A})$ simplifies by unit-propagation into $\mu^{\mathbf{A}} \wedge \chi(\mathbf{X}) \wedge \varphi(\mathbf{X})$, where $\mu^{\mathbf{A}} \overset{\text{def}}{=} \bigwedge_{n=0}^{N}(A_{n,l_n} \wedge \bigwedge_{l \neq l_n} \neg A_{n,l})$, and that $w_{[\mu^{\mathbf{A}}]}(\mathbf{X})$ simplifies into $w(\mathbf{X})$ because only one condition $(A_{n-1,l_{n-1}} \wedge A_{n,l_n})$ holds for the n-th external Case. This encoding allows us to answer the queries of interest as follows:

$$P(t_N \leq t_{\text{arr}} \mid t_0 = t_{\text{dep}}, l_{\text{dep}}, l_{\text{target}}, \text{next}) =$$
$$\frac{\text{WMI}(\varphi(\mathbf{X}, \mathbf{A}) \wedge \chi(\mathbf{X}, \mathbf{A}) \wedge (t_N \leq t_{\text{arr}}) \wedge (t_0 = t_{\text{dep}}), w(\mathbf{X}, \mathbf{A})|\mathbf{X}, \mathbf{A})}{\text{WMI}(\varphi(\mathbf{X}, \mathbf{A}) \wedge \chi(\mathbf{X}, \mathbf{A}) \wedge (t_0 = t_{\text{dep}}), w(\mathbf{X}, \mathbf{A})|\mathbf{X}, \mathbf{A})}$$

where l_{dep}, l_{target} and next are used to generate a query-specific encoding for $\varphi(\mathbf{X}, \mathbf{A})$, $\chi(\mathbf{X}, \mathbf{A})$ and $w(\mathbf{X}, \mathbf{A})$.

4.3.3 Efficiency of the encodings

Note that, with both encodings in 4.3.1 and 4.3.2, in the formula χ the constraints

$$[\![\text{OneOf}\{[\![t_{n-1} \in I^m]\!]\}_{m=1}^{M}]\!]$$

are not strictly necessary from the logical perspective because the I^m's are mutually exclusive by construction and $[\![t_n \in [c_1, c_{M+1}]]\!]$ for $n \in [0, N]$. Nevertheless, adding such constraints may improve the performances of the SMT solver the formula is fed to, because they allow the solver to infer the disjunction and the mutual exclusion directly via Boolean constraint propagation instead of using less efficient $\mathcal{LRA}$-deduction steps (see e.g. *static learning* in [95]).

For the same reason, adding the following logically-redundant constraints to χ may improve the performances of the SMT solver:

$$\left(\sum_{i=1}^{n-1} x_i + t_0 \geq c_{m+1}\right) \rightarrow \left(\sum_{i=1}^{n-1} x_i + t_0 \geq c_m\right) \quad \forall n \in [1, N], \ m \in [1, M-1]$$
$$(x_n \geq v_i) \rightarrow (x_n \geq v_j) \quad \text{if } v_i \geq v_j, \ \forall n \in [1, N],$$

where the v_i, v_j are among the upper- and lower-bound values of the intervals $R^m_{l_{n-1}, l_n}$. In practice, we do not need adding such constraints for every pair $\langle v_i, v_j \rangle$; rather and more efficiently, it suffices to sort all such values for each x_n, and to add one constraint only for pairs of consecutive values, because the others are obtained implicitly by transitivity.

4.4 Efficient WMI Computation

We address the problem of computing efficiently the WMI of a $\mathsf{FIUC}^{\mathcal{LRA}}$ weight function $w(\mathbf{X}, \mathbf{A})$, with support formula χ and set of conditions $\mathbf{\Psi}$, over a formula $\varphi(\mathbf{X}, \mathbf{A})$.

The first step (if needed) is a preprocessing step in which the problem is transformed by labelling all conditions $\mathbf{\Psi}$ with fresh Boolean atoms $\mathbf{B}$, as in Theorem 1. Let $\varphi^*, w^*, \mathbf{X}, \mathbf{A}^*$ be the result of such process, where

$$\varphi^* \stackrel{\text{def}}{=} \varphi \wedge \chi \wedge \bigwedge_{k=1}^{K} (B_k \iff \psi_k)$$

$$w^* \stackrel{\text{def}}{=} w[\mathbf{B} \leftarrow \mathbf{\Psi}]$$

$$\mathbf{A}^* \stackrel{\text{def}}{=} \mathbf{A} \cup \mathbf{B}$$

Consequently, for every $\mu^{\mathbf{A}^*}$, $w^*_{[\mu^{\mathbf{A}^*}]}$ is feasibly integrable on $\varphi^*_{[\mu^{\mathbf{A}^*}]}$.

Remark 4. Following up with remark 3, hereafter we assume w.l.o.g. that each Boolean atom in $\mathbf{A}$ occurs in $\varphi \wedge \chi$ or in $\mathbf{\Psi}$, so that every atom in $\mathbf{A}^*$ occurs in φ^*. Consequently, each truth assignment in $TTA(\varphi^*)$ assigns every atom in $\mathbf{A}^*$. The same assumption applies to $\exists \mathbf{X}.\varphi^*$. [3]

4.4.1 The Procedure WMI-AllSMT

Consider $\mu = \mu^{\mathbf{A}^*} \wedge \mu^{\mathcal{LRA}} \in TTA(\varphi^*)$. Then $\mu^{\mathcal{LRA}} \in TTA(\varphi^*_{[\mu^{\mathbf{A}^*}]})$, so that we can compute $\mathsf{WMI}_{\mathsf{nb}}(\mu^{\mathcal{LRA}}, w^*_{[\mu^{\mathbf{A}^*}]}|\mathbf{X})$. Combining Theorem 1 with Proposition 2 allows us to compute the WMI as follows:

$$\mathsf{WMI}(\varphi, w|\mathbf{X}, \mathbf{A}) \tag{4.29}$$
$$= \mathsf{WMI}(\varphi^*, w^*|\mathbf{X}, \mathbf{A}^*).$$
$$= \sum_{\mu^{\mathbf{A}^*} \wedge \mu^{\mathcal{LRA}} \in TTA(\varphi^*)} \mathsf{WMI}_{\mathsf{nb}}(\mu^{\mathcal{LRA}}, w^*_{[\mu^{\mathbf{A}^*}]}|\mathbf{X}).$$

The set $TTA(\varphi^*)$ is computed by an AllSMT procedure implemented on top of an SMT solver like MATHSAT5—i.e., as $TTA(\mathsf{PredAbs}_{[\varphi^*]}(Atoms(\varphi^*)))$, without the assignment-reduction technique (see fact (2) in section 4.1). Each $\mathsf{WMI}_{\mathsf{nb}}(\mu^{\mathcal{LRA}}, w^*_{[\mu^{\mathbf{A}^*}]}|\mathbf{X})$ is computed by invoking our background integration procedure for $\mathsf{FI}^{\mathcal{LRA}}$ functions of 4.2.3. We call this algorithm WMI-AllSMT.

---

[3]We note that this assumption is necessary for our basic procedure WMI-AllSMT (see 4.4.1) but it is not necessary with our much more efficient procedure WMI-PA (see 4.4.2) because the SMT-based procedure we use for computing predicate abstraction, $TTA(\mathsf{PredAbs}_{[\varphi]}(\mathbf{A}))$, allows forcing the branches even on atoms A_i which do not actually occur in the input formula φ. Nevertheless, this assumption makes the explanation simpler.

Algorithm 1 WMI-PA$(\varphi, w, \mathbf{X}, \mathbf{A})$

$\langle \varphi^*, w^*, \mathbf{A}^* \rangle \leftarrow \mathsf{LabelConditions}(\varphi, w, \mathbf{X}, \mathbf{A})$
$\mathcal{M}^{\mathbf{A}^*} \leftarrow \mathit{TTA}(\mathsf{PredAbs}_{[\varphi^*]}(\mathbf{A}^*))$
$vol \leftarrow 0$
for $\mu^{\mathbf{A}^*} \in \mathcal{M}^{\mathbf{A}^*}$ **do**
   $\mathsf{Simplify}(\varphi^*_{[\mu^{\mathbf{A}^*}]})$
   if $\mathsf{LiteralConjunction}(\varphi^*_{[\mu^{\mathbf{A}^*}]})$ **then**
      $vol \leftarrow vol + \mathsf{WMI}_{\mathsf{nb}}(\varphi^*_{[\mu^{\mathbf{A}^*}]}, w^*_{[\mu^{\mathbf{A}^*}]}|\mathbf{X})$
   else
      $\mathcal{M}^{\mathcal{LRA}} \leftarrow \mathit{TA}(\mathsf{PredAbs}_{[\varphi^*_{[\mu^{\mathbf{A}^*}]}]}(\mathit{Atoms}(\varphi^*_{[\mu^{\mathbf{A}^*}]})))$
      for $\mu^{\mathcal{LRA}} \in \mathcal{M}^{\mathcal{LRA}}$ **do**
         $vol \leftarrow vol + \mathsf{WMI}_{\mathsf{nb}}(\mu^{\mathcal{LRA}}, w^*_{[\mu^{\mathbf{A}^*}]}|\mathbf{X})$
return vol

4.4.2 The Procedure WMI-PA

A much more efficient technique, which we call WMI-PA because it exploits SMT-based predicate abstraction in its full pruning power rather than simply as AllSMT [4], can be implemented by noticing that, combining Theorem 1 with Proposition 3, we have that:

$$\mathsf{WMI}(\varphi, w|\mathbf{X}, \mathbf{A}) \tag{4.30}$$
$$= \quad \mathsf{WMI}(\varphi^*, w^*|\mathbf{X}, \mathbf{A}^*).$$
$$= \sum_{\mu^{\mathbf{A}^*} \in \mathit{TTA}(\exists \mathbf{X}.\varphi^*)} \mathsf{WMI}_{\mathsf{nb}}(\varphi^*_{[\mu^{\mathbf{A}^*}]}, w^*_{[\mu^{\mathbf{A}^*}]}|\mathbf{X})$$

and that, due to Proposition 1, each $\mathsf{WMI}_{\mathsf{nb}}(\varphi^*_{[\mu^{\mathbf{A}^*}]}, w^*_{[\mu^{\mathbf{A}^*}]}|\mathbf{X})$ can be computed as:

$$\sum_{\mu^{\mathcal{LRA}} \in \mathit{TA}(\varphi^*_{[\mu^{\mathbf{A}^*}]})} \mathsf{WMI}_{\mathsf{nb}}(\mu^{\mathcal{LRA}}, w^*_{[\mu^{\mathbf{A}^*}]}|\mathbf{X}). \tag{4.31}$$

Note that in (4.30) we must use $\mathit{TTA}(...)$ instead of $\mathit{TA}(...)$ because by construction $w^*_{[\mu^{\mathbf{A}^*}]}$ requires each $\mu^{\mathbf{A}^*}$ to be total, whereas in (4.31) we can use $\mathit{TA}(...)$ because there is no need for the $\mu^{\mathcal{LRA}}$s to be total (Proposition 1).

The pseudocode of WMI-PA is reported in Algorithm 1. First, the problem is transformed (if needed) by labelling conditions Ψ with fresh Boolean variables $\mathbf{B}$, as in Theorem 1. After this preprocessing stage, the set $\mathcal{M}^{\mathbf{A}^*} \stackrel{\mathrm{def}}{=} \mathit{TTA}(\exists \mathbf{X}.\varphi^*)$ is computed by invoking $\mathit{TTA}(\mathsf{PredAbs}_{[\varphi^*]}(\mathbf{A}^*))$ (see 4.1). Then, the algorithm iterates over each Boolean assignment $\mu^{\mathbf{A}^*}$ in $\mathcal{M}^{\mathbf{A}^*}$. $\varphi^*_{[\mu^{\mathbf{A}^*}]}$ can be simplified by the Simplify procedure, by propagating truth values (e.g., $\varphi_1 \wedge (\top \vee \varphi_2) \wedge (\bot \vee \varphi_3) \wedge (\neg \varphi_3 \vee \varphi_4) \Rightarrow \varphi_1 \wedge \varphi_3 \wedge \varphi_4$) and by applying arithmetical simplifications like $\mathcal{LRA}$ theory propagation [7] (e.g., $(x \geq 1) \wedge (\neg(x \geq 0) \vee \varphi_1) \wedge ((x \geq 0) \vee \varphi_2) \Rightarrow (x \geq 1) \wedge \varphi_1$). This improves the chances of reducing $\varphi^*_{[\mu^{\mathbf{A}^*}]}$ to a conjunction of

---

[4]To this extent, compare facts (3) and (2) in section 4.1.

literals, and allows reducing the size of $Atoms(\varphi^*_{[\mu A^*]})$ to feed to PredAbs (see below). Then, if $\varphi^*_{[\mu A^*]}$ is already a conjunction of literals, then the algorithm directly computes its contribution to the volume by calling $\mathsf{WMI}_{\mathsf{nb}}(\varphi^*_{[\mu A^*]}, w^*_{[\mu A^*]}|\mathbf{X})$. Otherwise, $\mathcal{TA}(\varphi^*_{[\mu A^*]})$ is computed as $\mathcal{TA}(\mathsf{PredAbs}_{[\varphi^*_{[\mu A^*]}]}(Atoms(\varphi^*_{[\mu A^*]})))$, using the assignment-reduction technique to produce partial assignments (see 2.3.1), and the algorithm iteratively computes the contributions to the volume for each $\mu^{\mathcal{LRA}}$.

Example 18. Consider the problem described by φ^* and w^* in Example 17. Since $\mathbf{A} = \varnothing$, then $\mathbf{A}^* = \mathbf{B}$.

Suppose first we generically want to leave l_0 no earlier than 7 and no later than 10, and arrive to l_2 strictly before 11. These constraints correspond to conjoining

$$[\![t_0 \in [7, 10)]\!] \wedge (t_0 + x_1 + x_2 < 11)$$

to φ^*. In such case, $\mathsf{PredAbs}_{[\varphi^*]}(\mathbf{A}^*)$ is the following formula:

$$(\ \ B_0^1 \wedge \neg B_0^2 \wedge \neg B_0^3 \wedge \ \ B_1^1 \wedge \neg B_1^2 \wedge \neg B_1^3) \tag{4.32}$$
$$\vee(\ \ B_0^1 \wedge \neg B_0^2 \wedge \neg B_0^3 \wedge \neg B_1^1 \wedge \ \ B_1^2 \wedge \neg B_1^3) \tag{4.33}$$
$$\vee(\neg B_0^1 \wedge \ \ B_0^2 \wedge \neg B_0^3 \wedge \neg B_1^1 \wedge \neg B_1^2 \wedge \ \ B_1^3) \tag{4.34}$$

so that $\mathcal{M}^{\mathbf{A}^*} \stackrel{\text{def}}{=} \mathcal{TTA}(\mathsf{PredAbs}_{[\varphi^*]}(\mathbf{A}^*))$ is the set of the three disjuncts (4.32)-(4.34). Importantly, note that the other 6 assignments, which would make φ^* $\mathcal{LRA}$-unsatisfiable causing $\mathsf{WMI}_{\mathsf{nb}}$ to return 0, *are not generated by* $\mathcal{TTA}(\mathsf{PredAbs}_{[\varphi^*]}(\mathbf{A}^*))$. (E.g., if $B_0^1 = \top$ then l_1 is necessarily reached strictly before 9, which forces $B_1^3 = \bot$, s.t. the assignment $(B_0^1 \wedge \neg B_0^2 \wedge \neg B_0^3 \wedge \neg B_1^1 \wedge \neg B_1^2 \wedge B_1^3)$ is not generated.)

Now suppose instead that we fix t_0 to some value $t_{\mathsf{dep}} \in [7, 10)$ by conjoining $(t_0 = t_{\mathsf{dep}})$ to φ^* (see 4.5). Depending on the value t_{dep}, we distinguish four cases:

- $t_{\mathsf{dep}} \in [7, 7.5)$: forces $B_0^1 = \top$ and $\mathcal{TTA}(\mathsf{PredAbs}_{[\varphi^*]}(\mathbf{A}^*))$ reduces to (4.32) and (4.33);

- $t_{\mathsf{dep}} \in [7.5, 8)$: forces $B_0^1 = \top$ and $\mathcal{TTA}(\mathsf{PredAbs}_{[\varphi^*]}(\mathbf{A}^*))$ reduces to (4.33) because (4.32) cannot be extended with any $\mathcal{LRA}$-satisfiable $\mu^{\mathcal{LRA}}$;

- $t_{\mathsf{dep}} \in [8, 9)$: forces $B_0^2 = \top$ and $\mathcal{TTA}(\mathsf{PredAbs}_{[\varphi^*]}(\mathbf{A}^*))$ reduces to (4.34);

- $t_{\mathsf{dep}} \in [9, 10)$: makes the whole formula $\mathcal{LRA}$-unsatisfiable, s.t. $\mathcal{TTA}(\mathsf{PredAbs}_{[\varphi^*]}(\mathbf{A}^*))$ is empty.

E.g., in the first case, if we set t_{dep} to 7.4 by conjoining $(t_0 = 7.4)$ to φ^*, then $\mathcal{TTA}(\mathsf{PredAbs}_{[\varphi^*]}(\mathbf{A}^*))$ contains only (4.32) and (4.33). Let (4.32) be the first assignment selected in the "for" loop, that is, $\mu^{\mathbf{A}^*} \stackrel{\text{def}}{=} (B_0^1 \wedge \neg B_0^2 \wedge \neg B_0^3 \wedge B_1^1 \wedge \neg B_1^2 \wedge \neg B_1^3)$. Propagating its truth values inside φ^* and w^* in (4.28) and (4.29) and simplifying the truth values by means of Simplify(), we get rid of most $\mathcal{LRA}$-literals in φ^*, obtaining thus: [5]

$$\varphi^*_{[\mu\mathbf{A}^*]} = (t_0 = 7.4) \wedge [\![t_0 \in [7, 10)]\!]$$
$$\wedge (t_0 + x_1 + x_2 < 11)$$
$$\wedge [\![t_0 \in [7, 8)]\!] \wedge [\![x_1 \in [0.5, 1)]\!]$$
$$\wedge [\![t_0 + x_1 \in [7, 8)]\!] \wedge [\![x_2 \in [1, 1.5)]\!]$$
$$w^*_{[\mu\mathbf{A}^*]} = f^1_{l_0 l_1}(x_1) \cdot f^1_{l_1 l_2}(x_2)$$

$\varphi^*_{[\mu\mathbf{A}^*]}$ is a conjunction of $\mathcal{LRA}$-literals, so that the condition of the "if" is verified, then $\mathsf{WMI_{nb}}$ can be invoked on it directly at the cost of one integration only, without further invoking another predicate abstraction and hence without running the internal "for", which would cost one integration for every internal loop.

4.4.3 WMI-PA vs. WMI-AllSMT

As a general remark, comparing (4.30) with (4.14) —even if $\varphi^*, w^*, \mathbf{X}, \mathbf{A}^*$ were respectively $\varphi, w, \mathbf{X}, \mathbf{A}$— we note that in WMI-PA the restriction of the sum to $\mathit{TTA}(\exists \mathbf{X}.\varphi^*)$ in (4.30) removes *a priori* all the assignments $\mu^{\mathbf{A}^*}$ which cannot be expanded by any assignment $\mu^{\mathcal{LRA}}$ s.t. $\mu^{\mathbf{A}^*} \wedge \mu^{\mathcal{LRA}}$ propositionally satisfies φ^* and $\mu^{\mathcal{LRA}}$ is $\mathcal{LRA}$-satisfiable, whose integrals would be 0-valued.

We argue that WMI-PA produces much less calls to the background integration procedure $\mathsf{WMI_{nb}}(\mu^{\mathcal{LRA}}, w^*_{[\mu\mathbf{A}^*]}|\mathbf{X})$ than WMI-AllSMT for two main reasons.

First, the size of $\mathit{Atoms}(\varphi^*_{[\mu\mathbf{A}^*]})$ which is fed to PredAbs in (4.31) can be made much smaller than the number of $\mathcal{LRA}$-atoms in $\mathit{Atoms}(\varphi^*)$ fed to PredAbs in (4.29), since many $\mathcal{LRA}$-atoms are simplified out by $\mu^{\mathbf{A}^*}$. (E.g., $((x \leq 1) \wedge (A_2 \vee (x \geq 0)))_{[A_2]}$ is simplified into $(x \leq 1)$, so that $(x \geq 0)$ is eliminated.) Thus, for each $\mu^{\mathbf{A}^*}$, the number of assignments in the form $\mu^{\mathbf{A}^*} \wedge \mu^{\mathcal{LRA}}$ which are enumerated in (4.30)-(4.31) can be drastically reduced with respect to those enumerated in (4.29).

Second, with (4.31) it is possible to search for a set $\mathit{TA}(...)$ of *partial* assignments, each of which substitutes 2^i total ones, i being the number of unassigned $\mathcal{LRA}$-atoms. Note that, unlike with Boolean atoms, we can safely produce partial assignments on $\mathcal{LRA}$-atoms because $w(\mathbf{X}, \mathbf{A})$ does not depend directly on them, since the integrals can be computed also on a partial assignment of the $\mathcal{LRA}$-atoms. (E.g., if $\varphi^*_{[\mu\mathbf{A}^*]} \overset{\text{def}}{=} (x \geq 0) \wedge ((x \leq 2) \vee (x \leq 1))$, the partial assignment $\mu^{\mathcal{LRA}} \overset{\text{def}}{=} (x \geq 0) \wedge (x \leq 2)$ prevents enumerating the two total ones $\mu^{\mathcal{LRA}} \wedge (x \leq 1)$ and $\mu^{\mathcal{LRA}} \wedge \neg(x \leq 1)$, computing one integral rather than two.

---

[5]Note that $[\![t_0 \in [7, 10)]\!]$ and $[\![t_0 \in [7, 8)]\!]$ are made redundant by $(t_0 = 7.4)$; however, they do not affect the result.

4.5 Experiments

We have evaluated the performance of WMI-PA on both synthetic (4.5.1) and real-world (4.5.2 and 4.5.3) problems, comparing it with WMI$_{old}$ techniques and alternative symbolic approaches. These problems have been chosen also because they can be suitably encoded to be fed to all tools under test; in particular, they are very naturally encoded into WMI$_{old}$ without the exponential blowup described in 4.2.4.

In our empirical evaluation we compared the following tools:

- WMI-BC is our re-implementation of the WMI$_{old}$ procedure in [10];

- WMI-ALLSMT and WMI-PA are our implementations of the procedures described in 4.4.1 and 4.4.2 respectively;

- SVE is the implementation of the algorithm in [93] provided by the authors, adapted in order to parse our input format;

- PRAiSE[6] is the implementation of Probabilistic Inference Modulo Theories [112] provided by the authors.

The implementations of WMI-BC, WMI-ALLSMT and WMI-PA use MATHSAT5 [7] [19] to perform SMT reasoning and LATTE INTEGRALE [8] [68] to compute integrals of polynomials. To perform internal manipulations of the weight components, we used SYMPY [9], a Python library for symbolic mathematics. The software implementation of all algorithms, as well as all data and scripts for replicating the experiments in this paper are publicly available online. [10]

All experiments were run on a Virtual Machine with 7 cores running at a frequency of 2.2 GHz and 94 GB of RAM. The timeout was set at 10,000 seconds for each ⟨query, tool⟩ job pair. Importantly, comparing the numerical results of the tests it turned out that, when terminating, all tools returned the same values on the same queries (modulo roundings).

4.5.1 Synthetic Setting

The synthetic setting is conceived in order to test the performance of the different tools on generic WMI problems. The setting we use here is more elaborate than the one we employed in [78], with the aim of making it more challenging for WMI-PA, in particular to force WMI-PA to enter more frequently its inner loop (the loop in the "else" case in Algorithm 1). Note however that the results in the simpler setting reported in [78] are qualitatively similar to the ones we report here, with an even more pronounced advantage of the WMI-based approaches over the symbolic alternatives.

In what follows, let $A^{\mathbb{B}}$ denote a random Boolean atom drawn from $\mathbf{A}$, let $A^{\mathbb{R}}$ denote a random $\mathcal{LRA}$-atom over variables in $\mathbf{X}$, let $A^{\mathbb{B}/\mathbb{R}}$ denote a random Boolean or $\mathcal{LRA}$-atom. In

---

[6]http://aic-sri-international.github.io/aic-praise/
[7]http://mathsat.fbk.eu/
[8]https://www.math.ucdavis.edu/~latte/
[9]http://www.sympy.org/
[10]https://github.com/unitn-sml/wmi-pa

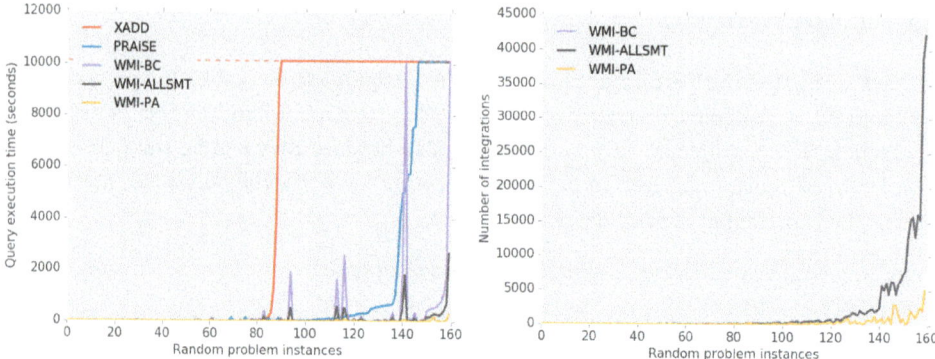

Figure 4.5: Query execution times in seconds for all methods on the synthetic experiment (left); number of integrals (right) for WMI-BC, WMI-ALLSMT and WMI-PA on the same instances.

this experiment, we used two recursive procedures to generate random formulas and nested weight functions with a given depth d:

$$\text{rand}_\varphi(d) = \begin{cases} \bigoplus_{q=1}^{Q} \text{rand}_\varphi(d-1) & \text{if } d > 0 \\ [\neg] A^{\mathbb{B}/\mathbb{R}} & \text{otherwise} \end{cases}$$

$$\text{rand}_w(d) = \begin{cases} [\![\text{If } \text{rand}_\varphi(d) \text{ Then } \text{rand}_w(d-1) \text{ Else } \text{rand}_w(d-1)]\!] \\ \text{or} \\ \text{rand}_w(d-1) \otimes \text{rand}_w(d-1) & \text{if } d > 0 \\ P_{\text{random}}(\mathbf{X}, max_{\text{deg}}) & \text{otherwise} \end{cases}$$

where $\bigoplus \in \{\vee, \wedge, \neg\vee, \neg\wedge\}$, $\otimes \in \{+, \cdot\}$ are randomly-picked Boolean and arithmetical operators respectively, "$[\neg]$" means that a negation is added at random, "w_1 or w_2" means that one of the two alternative functions w_1 and w_2 is chosen randomly, and $P_{\text{random}}(\mathbf{X}, max_{\text{deg}})$ are random polynomials over $\mathbf{X}$ with maximum degree max_{deg}.

Using the procedures above, we generated the problem instances as follows:

$$\chi(\mathbf{X}, \mathbf{A}) = \text{rand}_\varphi(D) \wedge \bigwedge_{x \in \mathbf{X}} [\![x \in [l_x, u_x]]\!]$$

$$w(\mathbf{X}, \mathbf{A}) = \text{rand}_w(D)$$

$$\varphi_{\text{query}}(\mathbf{X}, \mathbf{A}) = \text{rand}_\varphi(D)$$

where D is a parameter that control the depth of χ, w and φ_{query}, and $[l_x, u_x]$ are random lower and upper bounds for each variable $x \in \mathbf{X}$.

Figure 4.5 (left) shows the query execution times on the randomly generated problem instances for all the methods. Instances are ordered by increasing hardness, measured as the running time of the slowest method. For instances in which the slowest method reaches the

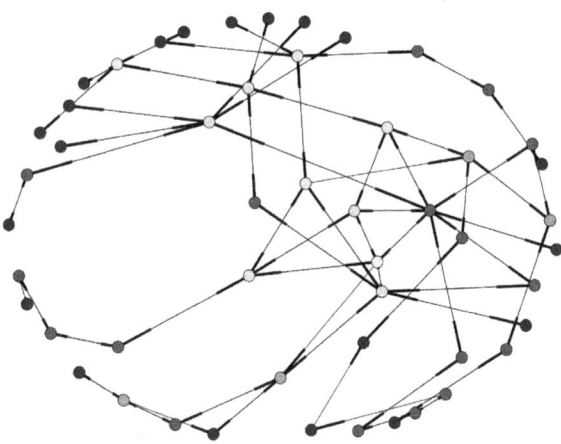

Figure 4.6: The subgraph of the Strategic Road Network used in our experiments. Locations are coloured according to their out degree.

timeout, the second slowest method is used to order instances, and so on. (Here and in next figures, a value of $10,000s$ denotes the fact that the procedure under test reached the timeout without producing a solution.)

In this experimental setting, the WMI methods achieve better performance with respect to the symbolic approaches, suggesting that the latter struggle with combinatorial reasoning, in contrast with the WMI approaches which rely on the full reasoning power of a state-of-the-art SMT solver.

Whereas WMI-ALLSMT performs better than the baseline WMI-BC for the most difficult cases, WMI-PA achieves drastic speedups with respect to both the alternatives. Figure 4.5 (right) reports the number of integrals computed by the three WMI methods. The curves for WMI-BC and WMI-ALLSMT are indistinguishable, an expected result as the two formulations enumerate the same set of total truth assignments, with WMI-ALLSMT doing it more efficiently. Conversely, the predicate abstraction steps of WMI-PA allow it to drastically reduce the number of assignments, and thus integrals to be computed. Note that a comparison with the symbolic approaches in terms of number of integrals is not possible because of their complex combination of variable elimination and integration steps.

4.5.2   Strategic Road Network with Fixed Path

In order to show the applicability of our method to real world tasks, we implemented the case study described in 4.3.1. The data was taken from the Strategic Road Network Dataset

[11], which provides a record of journey times on all the motorways managed by the English Highways Agency. From this dataset we extracted a graph between junctions whose edges were labelled with distributions of average journey times for each time interval (15 minutes long). For our experiments, we considered the largest strongly connected component of this graph, shown in Figure 4.6. In this setting, the task is to perform queries of the form:

$$P((t_N \leq t_{\text{arr}}) \mid t_0 = t_{\text{dep}}, \{l_i\}_{i=0}^{N}),$$

that is, computing the probability of completing a fixed path $l_1, ..., l_N$ within t_{arr}, given the departure time t_{dep}. We encoded an equivalent formulation for PRAiSE and compared it with the WMI approaches. SVE was not considered in this setting because its execution times are prohibitive for all but the smallest path lengths. Another issue we encountered with SVE is that it often runs out of memory due to the size of the underlying XADDs.

The results in Figure 4.7 show median, first and third quartiles of the query execution times, computed over 10 randomly generated queries for each path length. Whereas WMI-BC and WMI-ALLSMT cannot scale to the path lengths handled by PRAiSE, our approach is much faster than all alternatives, being able to compute queries up to two steps longer than PRAiSE without reaching the timeout.[12]

In contrast with the synthetic experiment, in this setting PRAiSE performs much better than WMI-BC and WMI-ALLSMT. On the one hand, PRAiSE seems to benefit from the deterministic relationships between the journey time variables, being able to symbolically decompose the integration much more efficiently with relation to the synthetic experiment, in which the continuous variables can relate to each other in diverse and entangled ways. On the other hand, the number of overlapping intervals in this encoding makes the enumeration of total truth assignments performed by WMI-BC and WMI-ALLSMT prohibitive (see 4.5.4).

Figure 4.8 shows the number of integrals computed by the three WMI techniques. (As before, this data cannot be provided with PRAiSE.) Note that the plots for WMI-BC and WMI-ALLSMT coincide, whereas that for WMI-PA cannot be distinguished from the x axis. From this, we observe that predicate abstraction techniques used in WMI-PA allow to drastically reduce the number of integrations.

4.5.3   Strategic Road Network with Conditional Plans

In order to further investigate the impact of combinatorial reasoning on the performance of WMI-PA and PRAiSE, we generalized the previous experiment to the case in which the path is not given in advance, using the encoding described in 4.3.2. In this experiment, we precomputed the conditional plan for each triple $\langle l_i, m, l_j \rangle$ using a greedy procedure based on expected journey time between adjacent locations. WMI-BC and WMI-ALLSMT were

---

[11]https://data.gov.uk/dataset/dft-eng-srn-routes-journey-times

[12]Note that the complexity of the query is due to the combination of the path length and the number of time intervals in which the time horizon is divided (M=12 in these experiments). For paths of length 8, the total number of potential cases is $12^8 = 429,981,696$. Clearly, most of these cases are unfeasible and are thus ruled out by the SMT solver before the integration.

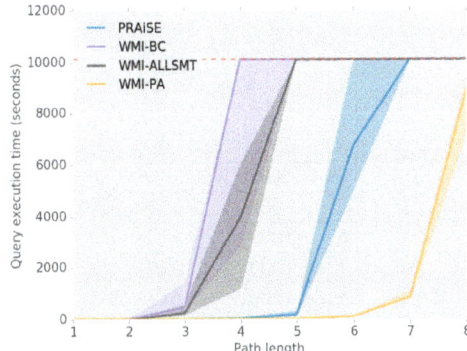

#	PRAiSE	WMI		
		BC	AllSMT	PA
1	2	1	0	0
2	3	10	8	0
3	7	425	253	0
4	22	> 10000	3994	2
5	174	> 10000	> 10000	8
6	6722	> 10000	> 10000	86
7	> 10000	> 10000	> 10000	850
8	> 10000	> 10000	> 10000	8884

Figure 4.7: Query execution times in seconds (1st quartile, median and 3rd quartile) in the Strategic Road Network setting with fixed path (left). Table showing the medians for each length (right).

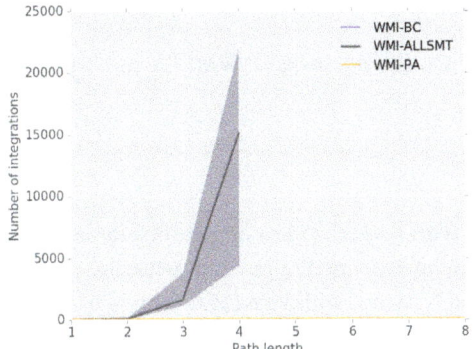

#	WMI		
	BC	AllSMT	PA
1	14	14	2
2	96	96	2
3	1653	1653	2
4	15105	15105	2
5	-	-	2
6	-	-	5
7	-	-	6
8	-	-	6

Figure 4.8: Number of integrations (1st quartile, median and 3rd quartile) computed by the WMI methods in the Strategic Road Network setting with fixed path (left). Table showing the medians for each method and path length (right).

not considered in this experiment, given their inability to scale on the simpler fixed path experiment. Recall that in this setting, the task is answering queries of the form:

$$P(t_N \leq t_{\text{arr}} \mid t_0 = t_{\text{dep}}, l_{\text{dep}}, l_{\text{target}}, \text{next}),$$

that is, computing the probability of reaching l_{target} within t_{arr}, leaving from l_{dep} at time t_{dep} and using the conditional plan encoded in next to make local decisions on the route to follow.

The results displayed in Figure 4.9 show that with the conditional-plan setting WMI-PA drastically outperforms PRAiSE, the performance gaps being even superior than that with the fixed-plan setting in Figure 4.7. [13] These results suggest that PRAiSE struggles with the heav-

[13]Comparing Figure 4.9 with Figure 4.7 one may got the (false) impression that the fixed plan problem is comparable or even harder for WMI-PA than the conditional-plan one. We note, however, that the two plots cannot be compared because in Figure 4.7 the x axis represents the length of the (fixed) plan whereas in Figure 4.9 it represents the *maximum* plan length, which can be bigger than the length of the actual plans.

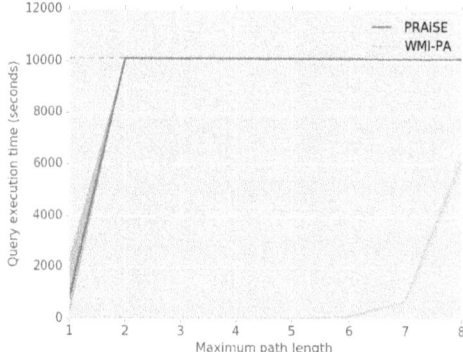

#	PRAiSE	WMI-PA
1	799	1
2	> 10000	2
3	> 10000	4
4	> 10000	6
5	> 10000	14
6	> 10000	77
7	> 10000	708
8	> 10000	6203

Figure 4.9: Query execution times in seconds (1st quartile, median and 3rd quartile) in the Strategic Road Network setting with conditional plan (left). Table showing the medians for each maximum length (right).

ier combinatorial aspect of this generalization. On the other hand, WMI-PA can prune the combinatorial space much more efficiently.

4.5.4 Discussion

The remarkable performance gaps of WMI-PA with respect to its competitors, in particular with respect to WMI-AllSMT and WMI-BC, can be explained in terms of what discussed in 4.4.3. In particular, we analyze the Strategic Road Network with Fixed Path setting of 4.5.2 by generalizing the scenario of Example 18. (In what follows we have omitted the literals from the query, which can simply be conjoined to each truth assignment.)

Consider $\varphi^*(\mathbf{X}, \mathbf{B})$ as in 4.3.1, and consider some $\mu^{\mathbf{A}^*} \in \mathcal{M}^{\mathbf{A}^*}$ as in Algorithm 1. Then, for every n, only one B_{n-1}^m is true (say, $B_{n-1}^{m_n}$) and all others are false in $\mu^{\mathbf{A}^*}$, so that $\bigwedge_{m=1}^M (B_{n-1}^m \iff [\![t_n \in I^m]\!])$ forces $[\![t_n \in I^{m_n}]\!]$ to be true and all the others to be false, so that $\bigwedge_{m=1}^M ([\![t_{n-1} \in I^m]\!] \to [\![x_n \in R_{l_{n-1},l_n}^m]\!])$ forces $[\![x_n \in R_{l_{n-1},l_n}^{m_n}]\!]$ to be true and satisfies all other constraints ($[\![t_{n-1} \in I^m]\!] \to [\![x_n \in R_{l_{n-1},l_n}^m]\!]$) for $m \neq m_n$, with no need to assign truth values to the other constraints $[\![x_n \in R_{l_{n-1},l_n}^m]\!]$.

With WMI-AllSMT (and WMI-BC) only *total* truth assignments $\mu^{\mathbf{A}^*} \wedge \mu^{\mathcal{LRA}}$ are generated from $\mathcal{TTA}(\varphi^*)$. We note that there can be up to $(2M-1)^N$ such assignments sharing the same $\mu^{\mathbf{A}^*}$ with different $\mu^{\mathcal{LRA}}$ part, each of which must be integrated separately. In fact, consider one $\mu^{\mathbf{A}^*}$ as above. WMI-AllSMT is forced to enumerate all total assignments $\mu^{\mathbf{A}^*} \wedge \mu_1^{\mathcal{LRA}}, \mu^{\mathbf{A}^*} \wedge \mu_2^{\mathcal{LRA}}, \dots$ extending $\mu^{\mathbf{A}^*}$ which cover all possible truth value combinations of the atoms in $[\![x_n \in R_{l_{n-1},l_n}^m]\!]$ with $m \neq m_n$ which are $\mathcal{LRA}$-consistent with $[\![x_n \in R_{l_{n-1},l_n}^{m_n}]\!]$, although a truth value assignment to these atoms is not necessary to satisfy the formula, as pointed out above. (Recall that the intervals $\{R_{l_{n-1},l_n}^m\}_m$ are not disjoint.) Depending on the possible overlappings of $R_{l_{n-1},l_n}^{m_n}$ with the other intervals R_{l_{n-1},l_n}^m with $m \neq m_n$, there are up to $(2M-1)^N$ such potential combinations: the extreme case is where, for every n, the bounds of the intervals R_{l_{n-1},l_n}^m are all different and for every $m \neq m_n$ $R_{l_{n-1},l_n}^m \subset R_{l_{n-1},l_n}^{m_n}$, so that $R^{mn}_{l_{n-1},l_n}$ is partitioned into $2M - 1$ sub-intervals, totaling $(2M - 1)^N$ combinations. We stress the fact that this partitioning is unnecessary because inside $R^{mn}_{l_{n-1},l_n}$ the weight function is not partitioned.

With WMI-PA, instead, the constraints $(\llbracket t_{n-1} \in I^m \rrbracket \rightarrow \llbracket x_n \in R^m_{l_{n-1},l_n} \rrbracket)$ for $m \neq m_n$ are removed from $\varphi^*_{[\mu^{\mathbf{A}^*}]}$ by Simplify(), so that $\varphi^*_{[\mu^{\mathbf{A}^*}]}$ is simplified into [14]

$$\bigwedge_{n=1}^{N} \left(\llbracket t_{n-1} \in I^{m_n} \rrbracket \wedge \bigwedge_{m=1}^{m_n-1} (t_{n-1} \geq c_m) \wedge \bigwedge_{m=m_n+1}^{M} \neg(t_{n-1} \geq c_{m-1}) \wedge \llbracket x_n \in R^{m_n}_{l_{n-1},l_n} \rrbracket \right)$$

which is a conjunction of $\mathcal{LRA}$-literals (namely $\mu^{\mathcal{LRA}}$). Thus, with the fixed-path setting, WMI-PA generates only one $\mu^{\mathcal{LRA}}$ to integrate for every $\mu^{\mathbf{A}^*} \in \mathcal{M}^{\mathbf{A}^*}$.

A direct theoretical comparison of the WMI techniques with respect to the symbolic techniques in SVE [93] and PRAISE [112] is not possible, because of the very different nature of such procedures—and of the fact that the code of PRAISE is much more complex and sophisticated than the general algorithm described in [112]—so that we limit to express a few conjectures.

Concerning the performance of SVE, we conjecture that its major limitation is that it requires to enumerate all paths from the root to the leaves in the XADD during computation, thus producing a blow-up both in memory requirements and number of alternatives to be evaluated.

An analysis of the performance difference between PRAISE and WMI-BC/WMI-AllSMT is more difficult. On the one hand, to the best of our understanding of the algorithm in [112], PRAISE supports some form of reasoning on partial $\mathcal{LRA}$-subassignments, which we conjecture to provide a good advantage with respect to WMI-BC and WMI-AllSMT on the road-network setting, where this feature is critical. On the other hand, where the above issue is less critical as with the synthetic setting, we conjecture that the usage of variable-elimination techniques might be less efficient than the Boolean decomposition plus numerical integrations, as done by WMI-BC and WMI-AllSMT.

Finally, when comparing PRAISE and WMI-PA—in addition to what mentioned in the last paragraph—we conjecture that the superiority in performance might be due mostly to the two-step usage of predicate abstraction interleaved with formula simplification, which allows both for getting rid of most $\mathcal{LRA}$-atoms from $\varphi^*_{[\mu^{\mathbf{A}^*}]}$ and for enumerating *partial* assignments on them, so that to drastically prune the number of $\mathcal{LRA}$-assignments $\mu^{\mathcal{LRA}}$ produced and thus the number of integrals performed.

---

[14]Recall from 4.3.1 that $\llbracket t_{n-1} \in I^{m_n} \rrbracket \overset{\text{def}}{=} (t_{n-1} \geq c_{m-1}) \wedge \neg(t_{n-1} \geq c_m)$; consequently, we have that $\neg\llbracket t_{n-1} \in I^{m_n} \rrbracket = \neg(t_{n-1} \geq c_{m-1}) \vee (t_{n-1} \geq c_m)$, which is simplified into $(t_{n-1} \geq c_m)$ if $m < m_n$ and into $\neg(t_{n-1} \geq c_{m-1})$ if $m > m_n$.

4.6   Final remarks

While the comparison in section 4.5 seems to suggest that solver-based approaches with numerical integration procedures are generally superior, this is not always the case. In fact, SVE was later improved with caching techniques in [50], showing superior performance with respect to WMI-PA in a range of synthetic WMI problems. Moreover, symbolic approaches have the advantage of being generally more flexible with respect to solver-based approaches. For instance, symbolic solvers can return partial WMI computations [50] and different solving schemes can be easily combined [49]. Symbolic approaches also shine whenever computations can be reused for answering multiple queries, as reported both in section 5.4 and in [50]. In order to implement this feature in solver-based approaches, a much more complex interaction with a stack-based incremental SMT solver has to be realized.

The major limitation of WMI-PA is its inability to automatically decompose the integral whenever possible. This aspect hinders the use of this algorithm in high-dimensional scenarios. Currently, the algorithm requires total truth assignments to the conditions of the weight function, but this is often unnecessary for many densities of practical interest. Lifting this requirement is another promising research direction. Hybridisation of solver-based approaches with symbolic or approximate integration procedures is also currently being investigated.

CHAPTER 5

MP-MI

While relevant for some applications, the improvement to solver-based approaches described in the previous chapter does not achieve scalable WMI inference to high-dimensional settings. This motivated the study of the theoretical aspects of WMI inference. This chapter is based on a recent effort to trace the tractability boundaries of WMI problems [110] and provide the hybrid equivalent of the Belief Propagation (BP) algorithm (refer to section 2.1 for a description of BP on factor graphs).

Recently, [109] showed that a WMI problem can be reduced in poly-time to a Model Integration (MI) problem over continuous variables only. This reduction is appealing because it allows us to cast hybrid probabilistic reasoning with logical constraints in terms of volume computations over polytopes. In the following chapter we focus on the undirected case, although a more recent work that extends our findings to the weighted case and further expand the tractability bounderies is currently under revision.

Our theoretical analysis and the message passing algorithm are based on the concept of *primal graph*, a graphical structure that encodes the dependencies between variables of a WMI problem. Both primal graphs and the reduction to the unweighted case are described in section 5.1. Section 5.2 provides an analysis of the hardness of MI problems. Tracing the boundaries of tractability is not only relevant from a theoretical standpoint, but it also has practical utility in characterizing the problems that can be efficiently solved, thus suggesting an algorithm for tractable inference. The algorithm, dubbed MP-MI, allows the efficient computation of marginal densities and statistical moments of all the variables in linear time. As such, it is possible to amortize inference for rich MI queries when they conform to the dependency structure. Section 5.3 presents MP-MI, followed by a preliminary evaluation of its performance on synthetic data in section 5.4.

5.1 Preliminaries

Definition 7. In order to characterize the dependency structure of an SMT-$\mathcal{LRA}$ formula φ as well as the hardness of inference, we denote the *primal graph* [26] of formula φ by $\mathcal{G}_\varphi$, as the undirected graph whose vertices are variables in φ and whose edges connect any two variables that appear together in at least one clause in φ.

In the next sections, we will extensively refer to the *diameter* and *treewidth* of a primal graph defined as usual for undirected graphs [53].

We now briefly review the poly-time reduction from WMI to MI. We refer the readers to [109] for a detailed exposition.

First, without loss of generality, a WMI problem on continuous and Boolean variables of the form $\text{WMI}(\varphi, w|\mathbf{X}, \mathbf{A})$ can always be reduced to new WMI problem $\text{WMI}_{nb}(\varphi', w'|\mathbf{X}')$ on continuous variables only. To do so, we substitute the Boolean variables $\mathbf{A}$ in formula φ with fresh continuous variables in $\mathbf{X}'$ and replace each Boolean atom and its negation in formula φ by two exclusive $\mathcal{LRA}$ atoms over the new real variables in formula φ', and distilling a new weight function w accordingly. Note that the primal graph of formula φ' retains its treewidth, i.e., if primal graph $\mathcal{G}_\varphi$ is a tree, then so is the graph $\mathcal{G}_{\varphi'}$.

Furthermore, WMI problems on continuous variables with polynomial weights can be reduced to equivalent MI problems whose definition will be formally presented in the next paragraph. Specifically, WMI_{nb} with polynomial weights w' have equivalent MI problems $\text{WMI}_{nb}(\varphi', w'|\mathbf{X}') = \text{MI}(\varphi''|\mathbf{X}'')$, with $\mathbf{X}''$ containing auxiliary continuous variables whose extrema of integration are chosen such that their integration is precisely the value of weights w'.

$$\varphi = \begin{cases} \Gamma_1 : 0 < X_1 < 2 \\ \Gamma_2 : 0 < X_2 < 2 \\ \Gamma_3 : X_1 + X_2 < 2 \\ \Gamma_4 : B \vee (X_1 > 1) \end{cases} \qquad \varphi' = \begin{cases} \Gamma_1 : 0 < X_1 < 2 \\ \Gamma_2 : 0 < X_2 < 2 \\ \Gamma_3 : X_1 + X_2 < 2 \\ \Gamma_B : -1 < Z_B < 1 \\ \Gamma_4' : (0 < Z_B) \\ \qquad \vee (X_1 > 1) \end{cases} \qquad \varphi'' = \begin{cases} \varphi' \\ \Gamma_5 : 0 < Z'_{X_1} < X_1 \\ \Gamma_6 : 0 < Z_{X_2} < X_2 \\ \Gamma_7 : 0 < Z''_{X_1} < 2 \end{cases}$$

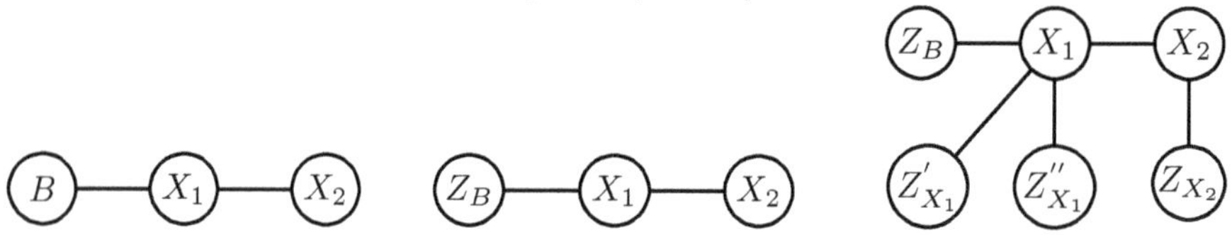

Figure 5.1: **From WMI to MI, passing by** WMI_{nb}. An example of a WMI problem with an SMT$\mathcal{LRA}$ CNF formula φ over real variables $\mathbf{X} = \{X_1, X_2\}$ and Boolean variable B and corresponding primal graph $\mathcal{G}_\varphi$ in (a). Their reductions to φ' and $\mathcal{G}_{\varphi'}$ as an WMI_{nb} problem in (b). The equivalent MI problem with formula φ'' and primal graph $\mathcal{G}_{\varphi''}$ over only real variables $\mathbf{X}'' = \mathbf{X} \cup \{Z_B, Z_{X_1}, Z_{X_2}\}$ after the introduction of auxiliary variables Z_B, Z_{X_1}, Z_{X_2}. Note that $\mathcal{G}_\varphi$ and $\mathcal{G}'_\varphi$ have the same treewidth one.

Example 19. Figure 5.1 illustrates one example of a reduction of a WMI problem to one WMI_{nb} one to a MI problem. Consider the WMI problem over formula $\varphi = (0 < X_1 < 2) \wedge (0 < X_2 < 2) \wedge (X_1 + X_2 < 1) \wedge (B \vee (X_1 > 1))$ on variables $\mathbf{X} = \{X_1, X_2\}, \mathbf{A} = \{B\}$ whose primal graph $\mathcal{G}_\varphi$ is also shown in figure 5.1 (left). Assume a weight function which decomposes as

$$w(X_1, X_2, B) = w_a(X_1, X_2) \cdot w_b(X_1) \cdot w_c(B)$$
$$w_a(X_1, X_2) = X_1 \cdot X_2$$
$$w_b(X_1) = [\![\text{If } (X_1 > 1) \text{ Then 2 Else 1}]\!]$$
$$w_c(B) = [\![\text{If } B \text{ Then 3 Else 1}]\!]$$

The WMI of formula φ is:

$$\text{WMI}(\varphi, w; \mathbf{X}, \{B\}) = \int_0^1 dx_1 \int_0^{2-x_1} 1 \times 3x_1 x_2 \, dx_2 \tag{5.1}$$
$$+ \int_1^2 dx_1 \int_0^{2-x_1} 2 \times 3x_1 x_2 \, dx_2$$
$$+ \int_1^2 dx_1 \int_0^{2-x_1} 2 \times 1x_1 x_2 \, dx_2 \ .$$

In figure 5.1 (center) we show the reduction to the above example problem to a WMI$_{\text{nb}}$ one. A free real variable Z_B is introduced to replace Boolean variable B. Then, the equivalent problem to the WMI one in Equation 5.1, can be computed as:

$$\text{WMI}_{\text{nb}}(\varphi', w') = \int_0^1 dz_B \int_0^1 dx_1 \int_0^{2-x_1} 1 \times 3x_1 x_2 \, dx_2 \tag{5.2}$$
$$+ \int_0^1 dz_B \int_1^2 dx_1 \int_0^{2-x_1} 2 \times 3x_1 x_2 \, dx_2$$
$$+ \int_{-1}^0 dz_B \int_1^2 dx_1 \int_0^{2-x_1} 2 \times 1x_1 x_2 \, dx_2 \ .$$

Figure 5.1 (right) illustrates the additional reduction from the above WMI$_{\text{nb}}$ problem to a MI one. There, additional real variables Z'_{X_1}, Z_{X_2} and Z''_{X_1} are added to formula φ'' in substitution of the monomial weights attached to literals. Therefore, the same result as Equation 5.1 and Equation 5.2 can be obtained as

$$\text{MI}(\varphi'') = \int_0^3 dz_B \int_0^1 dx_1 \int_0^{2-x_1} dx_2 \int_0^{x_1} dz'_{X_1} \int_0^{x_2} dz_{X_2} \tag{5.3}$$
$$+ \int_0^2 dz''_{X_1} \int_0^3 dz_B \int_1^2 dx_1 \int_0^{2-x_1} dx_2 \int_0^{x_1} dz'_{X_1} \int_0^{x_2} dz_{X_2}$$
$$+ \int_0^2 dz''_{X_1} \int_1^2 dx_1 \int_0^{2-x_1} dx_2 \int_0^{x_1} dz'_{X_1} \int_0^{x_2} dz_{X_2} \ .$$

In the case of monomial weights, the treewidth of $\mathcal{G}''_\varphi$ will not increase w.r.t. $\mathcal{G}'_\varphi$. This is not guaranteed for generic polynomial weights. For a detailed description of these reduction processes refer to [110].

5.1.1 Computing MI

Given a set $\mathbf{X}$ of continuous random variables over $\mathbb{R}$, and an SMT-$\mathcal{LRA}$ formula $\Delta = \bigwedge_i \Gamma_i$ over $\mathbf{X}$, the task of MI over formula φ, w.r.t. variables $\mathbf{X}$ is defined as computing the following integral [109]:

$$\mathrm{MI}(\varphi|\mathbf{X}) \stackrel{\text{def}}{=} \int_{\boldsymbol{x}\models\varphi} 1 \; d\boldsymbol{x} = \int_{\mathbb{R}^{|\mathbf{X}|}} [\![\boldsymbol{x} \models \varphi]\!] \; d\boldsymbol{x} = \int_{\mathbb{R}^{|\mathbf{X}|}} \prod_{\Gamma \in \varphi} [\![\boldsymbol{x} \models \Gamma]\!] \; d\boldsymbol{x}. \tag{5.4}$$

The first equality can be seen as computing the volume of the constrained regions defined by formula φ, and the last one is obtained by eliciting the "pieces" associated to each clause $\Gamma \in \varphi$. Again, in the following we will use the shorthand $\mathrm{MI}(\varphi)$ when integrating over all variables in formula φ. Moreover, the problem $\mathrm{MI}(\varphi)$ can be rewritten in an iterated integral form as follows:

$$\mathrm{MI}(\varphi) = \int_{\mathbb{R}} dx_1 \cdots \int_{\mathbb{R}} dx_{i-1} \int_{\mathbb{R}} f_i(x_i) \; dx_i, \quad i = 2, \cdots, n. \tag{5.5}$$

In a general way, we can always define a univariate piecewise polynomial f_i as a function of the MI over the remaining variables in a recursive way as follow:

$$f_i(x_i) = \int_{\mathbb{R}} [\![x_i, x_{i+1} \models \tilde{\varphi}_i]\!] \cdot f_{i+1}(x_{i+1}) \; dx_{i+1}, \; i \in [1, n-1] \qquad f_n(x_n) = [\![x_n \models \tilde{\varphi}_n]\!]$$

where the formula $\tilde{\varphi}_i = \exists \boldsymbol{x}_{1:i-1}.\varphi$. Recall that the formula φ is defined by SMT-$\mathcal{LRA}$ which means that the integration bounds are linear arithmetic over the real variables. Thus the MI can be expressed as the integration over an arbitrary variable $X_r \in \mathbf{X}$ where the integrand f_r is a univariate piecewise polynomial and the pieces are the collection I of intervals of the form $[l, u]$:

$$\mathrm{MI}(\varphi) = \int_{\mathbb{R}} f_r(x_r) \; dx_r = \sum_{[l,u] \in I} \int_l^u f_{l,u}(x_r) dx_r. \tag{5.6}$$

5.1.2 Hybrid inference via MI

Before moving to our theoretical and algorithmic contributions, we review the kind of probabilistic queries computable via MI.[1] Analogously to WMI(Δ, w), MI(φ) computes the partition function of the unnormalized distribution induced over the models of formula φ. Therefore, it is possible to compute the (now normalized) probability of any logical *query* Φ expressable as an SMT-$\mathcal{LRA}$ formula involving complex logical and numerical constraints as

$$P_\varphi(\Phi) = \mathrm{MI}(\varphi \wedge \Phi) \; / \; \mathrm{MI}(\varphi).$$

In the next section, we will show how to compute the probabilities of a collection of rich queries $\{\Phi_t\}_t$ in a single message-passing evaluation if all Φ_t are univariate formulas, i.e., contain only one variable $X_i \in \mathbf{X}$, or bivariate ones conforming to graph $\mathcal{G}_\varphi$, i.e., Φ_t contains

---

[1]Note that equivalent queries can be defined for WMI and WMI$_{\text{nb}}$ problem formulations.

only $X_i, X_j \in \mathbf{X}$ and they are connected by at least one edge in $\mathcal{G}_\varphi$. Moreover, one might want to statistically reason about the marginal distribution of the variables in $\mathbf{X}$, i.e., $p_\varphi(x_i)$ which is defined as:

$$P_\varphi(x_i) \overset{\text{def}}{=} \frac{1}{\text{MI}(\varphi)} f_i(x_i) = \frac{1}{\text{MI}(\varphi)} \int_{\mathbb{R}^{|\mathbf{X}|-1}} [\![\boldsymbol{x} \models \varphi]\!] \, d\boldsymbol{x} \setminus \{x_i\}. \tag{5.7}$$

5.2   On the inherent hardness of MI

It is well-known that for discrete probabilistic graphical models, the simplest structural requirement to guarantee tractable inference is to bound their treewidth [53]. For instance, for
tree-shaped Bayesian Networks, all exact marginals can be computed at once in polynomial
time [82]. However, existing WMI solvers show exponential blow-up in their runtime even
when the WMI problems have primal graphs with simple tree structures [109]. This obser-
vation motivates us to trace the theoretical boundaries for tractable probabilistic inference
via MI. As we will show in this section, we find out that requiring a MI problem to only
have a tree-shaped structure is not sufficient to ensure tractability. Therefore, inference on
MI problems is inherently harder than its discrete-only counterpart.

Specifically, we will show how the hardness of MI depends on two structural properties: the
treewidth of the primal graph and the length of its diameter. To begin, we prove that even
for SMT-$\mathcal{LRA}$ formulas φ whose primal graphs $\mathcal{G}_\varphi$ are trees but have unbounded diameters
(i.e., they are unbalanced trees, like paths), computing $\text{MI}(\varphi)$ is hard. This is surprising since
for its discrete counterpart, the complexity of model counting problem is exponential in the
treewidth but not in the diameter.

Theorem 2. Computing $\text{MI}(\varphi)$ of an SMT-$\mathcal{LRA}$ formula φ whose primal graph over n variables is a tree with diameter $\Theta(n)$ is #P-hard.

Proof. We prove our complexity result by reducing a #P-complete variant of the subset sum
problem [33] to an MI problem over an SMT-$\mathcal{LRA}$ theory φ with a tree primal graph whose
diameter is $\mathcal{O}(n)$. This problem is a counting version of the subset sum problem saying that
given a set of positive integers $S = \{s_0, s_1, \cdots, s_{n-1}\}$, and a positive integer L, the goal is
to count the number of subsets $S' \subseteq S$ such that the sum of all the integers in the subset S'
equals to L.

In a nutshell, one can always construct in polynomial time a theory φ such that its primal
graph $\mathcal{G}_\varphi$ is a chain (hence has $\Theta(n)$ diameter) and where computing $\text{MI}(\varphi)$ equals solving
(up to a constant) the aforementioned subset sum problem variant, which is known to be
#P-hard [23, 16]. Firstly, we reduce the counting subset sum problem in polynomial time to
a model integration problem with the following SMT-$\mathcal{LRA}$ theory whose primal graph is
shown in figure 5.2.

$$\Delta = \begin{cases} (-\frac{1}{2n} < X_1 - s_1 < \frac{1}{2n}) \vee (-\frac{1}{2n} < X_1 < \frac{1}{2n}) \\ (-\frac{1}{2n} < X_i - X_{i-1} - s_i < \frac{1}{2n}) \vee (-\frac{1}{2n} < X_i - X_{i-1} < \frac{1}{2n}), \quad i = 2, \cdots n \end{cases}$$

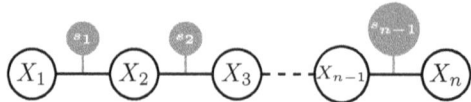

Figure 5.2: Primal graph used for #P-hardness reduction

For brevity, denote the first and the second literal in the i-th clause by $\ell(i,0)$ and $\ell(i,1)$, respectively. Also we choose two constants $l = L - \frac{1}{2}$ and $u = L + \frac{1}{2}$. In the following, we prove that $n^n \mathrm{MI}(\Delta \wedge (l < X_n < u))$ equals the number of subset $S' \subseteq S$ whose element sum is L.

Let $va^k = (a_1, a_2, \cdots, a_k)$ be some assignment to Boolean variables $\{A_1, A_2, \cdots, A_k\}$ with $a_i \in \{0,1\}$, $i \in [k]$. Define $S(va^k) \overset{\text{def}}{=} \sum_{i=1}^k a_i s_{i-1}$ as subset sums, and formulas $\Delta_{va^k} \overset{\text{def}}{=} \bigwedge_{i=1}^k \ell(i, a_i)$ for each va^k.

We claim that given an assignment $va^k \in \{0,1\}^k$, the model integration for theory Δ_{va^k} is $(\frac{1}{n})^k$. Moreover, using induction we conclude that for each variable x_i in Δ_{va^k}, its satisfying assignments form the interval $[\sum_{j=1}^i a_j s_{j-1} - \frac{i}{2n}, \sum_{j=1}^i a_j s_{j-1} + \frac{i}{2n}]$. Specifically, the satisfying assignments for variable x_n in theory Δ_{va^n} is the interval $[S(va^n) - \frac{1}{2}, S(va^n) + \frac{1}{2}]$. For any subset $S' \subseteq S$, we can have one-to-one correspondence to assignments in $\{0,1\}^n$ by defining va^n as $a_i = 1$ if and only if $s_i \in S'$. Furthermore, each assignments $va^n \in \{0,1\}^n$, the model integration of $\Delta_{va^n} \wedge (l < X_n < u)$ falls into one of the following two cases: 1) if $S(va^n) < L$ or $S(va^n) > L$, then $\mathrm{MI}(\Delta_{va^n} \wedge (l < X_n < u)) = 0$; 2) otherwise if $S(va^n) = L$, then $\mathrm{MI}(\Delta_{va^n} \wedge (l < X_n < u)) = (\frac{1}{n})^n$. Indeed, we have shown that variable X_n has its satisfying assignments in interval $[S(va^n) - \frac{1}{2}, S(va^n) + \frac{1}{2}]$ in theory Δ_{va^n} for each $va^n \in \{0,1\}^n$. If $S(va^n) < L$, given that $S(va^n)$ is a sum of positive integers, then it holds that $S(va^n) + \frac{1}{2} \le (L-1) + \frac{1}{2} = L - \frac{1}{2} = l$ and therefore, $\mathrm{MI}(\Delta_{va^n} \wedge (l < X_n < u)) = 0$; similarly, if $S(va^n) > L$, then it holds that $S(va^n) - \frac{1}{2} \ge u$ and therefore, $\mathrm{MI}(\Delta_{va^n} \wedge (l < X_n < u)) = 0$. If $S(va^n) = L$, we have $\mathrm{MI}(\Delta_{va^n} \wedge (l < X_n < u)) = \mathrm{MI}(\Delta_{va^n}) = (\frac{1}{n})^n$.

Observe that for each clause in SMT-$\mathcal{LRA}$ Δ, literals are mutually exclusive since each s_i is a positive integer. Then we have that formulas Δ_{va^n} are mutually exclusive and meanwhile $\Delta = \bigvee_{va^n} \Delta_{va^n}$. Thus it holds that $\mathrm{MI}(\Delta) = \sum_{va^n} \mathrm{MI}(\Delta_{va^n})$. Similarly, we have formulas $(\Delta_{va^n} \wedge (l < X_n < u))$'s are mutually exclusive and meanwhile $\mathrm{MI}(\Delta \wedge (l < X_n < u)) = \sum_{va^n} \mathrm{MI}(\Delta_{va^n} \wedge (l < X_n < u))$. From the above results, we can conclude that $\mathrm{MI}(\Delta \wedge (l < X_n < u)) = t(\frac{1}{n})^n$ where t is the number of assignments va^n such that $S(va^n) = L$. Notice that for each $va^n \in \{0,1\}^n$, it one-to-one corresponds to a subset $S' \subseteq S$ and $S(va^n)$ equals to L if and only if the sum of elements in S' is L. This finishes our proof of the statement that $n^n \mathrm{MI}(\Delta \wedge (l < X_n < u))$ equals to the number of subset $S' \subseteq S$ whose element sum equals to L. Therefore, model integration problems with tree primal graphs whose diameter is $\mathcal{O}(n)$ is #P-hard. $\square$

Furthermore, when the primal graphs are balanced trees, i.e., they have $O(\log(n))$ diameters, increasing their treewidth from one to two is sufficient to turn MI problems from tractable to #P-hard.

Theorem 3. Computing $MI(\varphi)$ of an SMT-$\mathcal{LRA}$ formula φ whose primal graph $\mathcal{G}_\varphi$ has treewidth two is #P-hard, with n being the number of variables.

Proof. [Sketch of proof] As before, we construct a poly-time reduction from the #P-complete variant of the subset sum problem to an MI problem. This time, the SMT-$\mathcal{LRA}$ formula φ is built such that the graph $\mathcal{G}_\varphi$ has treewidth two with cliques (hence not a tree). Meanwhile the primal graph has diameter to be at most $\log(n)$ by putting the cliques in a balanced way. Then the MI over a subtree could potentially be a subset sum over the integers that appear in the formulas associated with the subtree. Then computing the MI of formula φ equals to solving the subset sum problem. For the complete proof, refer to [110]. □

From Theorems 2 and 3 we can deduce that having a tree-shaped *and* balanced primal graph is a necessary condition for tractability. Together with the fact that our proposed exact MI solver, which will be introduce in the next section, achieves quasi-polynomial complexity on MI with balanced tree-shaped primal graphs, we shows that the balanced tree-shape is both necessary and sufficient. This sets the standard for the solver complexity: every exact MI solver that aims to be efficient, need to operate in the aforementioned regime.

In next section we introduce a novel and efficient exact MI solver on MI with balanced tree-shaped primal graphs together with its complexity analysis. It computes exact MI by exchanging messages among the nodes of the primal graph of an SMT-$\mathcal{LRA}$ formula. As the reader might guess at this point, devising a message passing inference scheme for MI will be inherently more challenging than for discrete domains.

From the previous section we know that MI actually can be viewed as integration over univariate piecewise polynomials. Piecewise polynomials are universal and compact representations that are closed under multiplication, addition, marginalization and conditioning on evidence. This will allow us to distill a message passing scheme where both messages and beliefs are still in the univariate piecewise polynomial family.

When operating on primal graphs that are trees, our MI via message passing will be exact. The belief update is done in a upward-and-downward manner and by performing it one can directly obtain the marginals for each node – the same nice property as its only-discrete and only-continuous counterparts [53, 82]. Besides doing model integration, the stored beliefs will allow us to amortize computations for multiple queries on SMT-$\mathcal{LRA}$ formulas, at inference time.

5.3 MP-MI: exact MI inference via message passing

Deriving an equivalent message passing scheme for MI to what belief propagation is for the discrete case [82] poses unique and considerable challenges. First, by allowing complex logical constraints such as those creating disjoint feasible regions, one might have to integrate over exponentially many polytopes. This is computationally expensive even though numerical integration is a consolidated field. Additionally, different from discrete domains, in real or hybrid domains one generally does not have universal and compact representations for

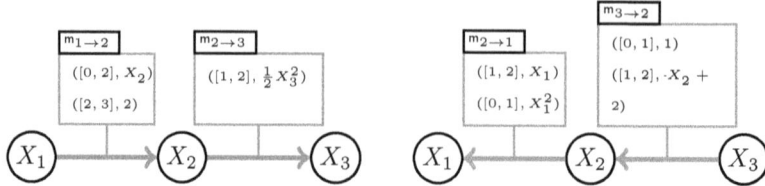

Figure 5.3: **An example of a run of MP-MI**. Upward (blue) and downward (pink) messages are shown as piecewise polynomials in boxes for a tree primal graph rooted at X_3. The final belief for X_2 can then be computed as the piecewise polynomial $b_2 = m_{1 \to 2} \cdot m_{3 \to 2} = \{([0, 1], X_2), ([1, 2], -X_2^2 + 2X_2)\}$.

distributions [53, 102]. And when these are available, e.g. in the case of Gaussians, the corresponding density models might have restricted expressiveness and not allow for efficient integration over arbitrary constraints. In fact, in the case of exponentiated polynomials, exact integration of is limited to polynomials of low degree (usually, two).

5.3.1   Propagation scheme

In what follows we describe a message passing scheme for MI problems with tree-shaped primal graphs.

Let φ be an SMT-$\mathcal{LRA}$ formula and $\mathcal{G}_\varphi$ its tree primal graph, rooted at node r corresponding to variable $X_r \in \mathbf{X}$. This can always be done by choosing an arbitrary node r as root and then orienting all edges away from node r.

Also let $\mathcal{V}$ be the set of indexes of variables $\mathbf{X}$ in formula φ and let $\mathcal{E}$ be the set of edges $i - j$ in graph $\mathcal{G}_\varphi$ connecting variables X_i and X_j. Then the formula can be rewritten as $\varphi = \bigwedge_{i \in \mathcal{V}} \varphi_i \wedge \bigwedge_{(i,j) \in \mathcal{E}} \varphi_{i,j}$, with φ_i being formulas involving only variable X_i and, analogously, formula $\varphi_{i,j}$ involving only variables X_i and X_j. Notice that the tree primal graph assumption implies that each clause in the formula has at most two variables; otherwise if there are more than two variables in one clause, these variables would be pairwise connected by one edge in the primal graph and create loops.

Our inference scheme, which we name MP-MI, will be able to compute the unnormalized marginals of each node in $\mathcal{G}_\varphi$, defining the *belief* associated to that node.

Definition 8. Let φ be an SMT-$\mathcal{LRA}$ formula with tree primal graph $\mathcal{G}_\varphi$. The *belief* b_i of node i in graph $\mathcal{G}_\varphi$ is the unnormalized marginal $p_i(x_i)$ of variable $X_i \in \mathbf{X}$.

As we will show, in MP-MI beliefs can be computed by exchanging *messages* between nodes in $\mathcal{G}_\varphi$.

Definition 9. The message from a node i (corresponding to variable $X_i \in \mathbf{X}$) in primal graph

$\mathcal{G}_\varphi$ to one of its neighbor nodes $j \in \text{neigh}(i)$ is computed recursively as follows,

$$m_{i \to j}(x_j) = \int_\mathbb{R} [\![x_i, x_j \models \varphi_{i,j}]\!][\![x_i \models \varphi_i]\!] \times \prod\nolimits_{c \in \text{neigh}(i) \setminus \{j\}} m_{c \to i}(x_i) \, dx_i \qquad (5.8)$$

MP-MI operates in two phases: an *upward pass* and a *downward* one. First we send messages up from the leaves to the root (upward pass) such that each node has all information from its children and then we incorporate messages from the root down to the leaves (downward pass) such that each node also has information from its parent node. When the message passing process finishes, each node in graph $\mathcal{G}_\varphi$ is able to compute its belief by aggregating the messages received from all its neighbors.

Proposition 4. Let $\text{ch}(i)$ be the set of children nodes for node i in $\mathcal{G}_\varphi$. The belief of node i in the upward pass, b_i^{up}, and the downward belief b_i^{down}, can be computed as:

$$b_i^{\text{up}}(x_i) = \prod_{c \in \text{ch}(i)} m_{c \to i}(x_i), \quad b_i(x_i) = b_i^{\text{down}}(x_i) = \prod_{c \in \text{neigh}(i)} m_{c \to i}(x_i) \qquad (5.9)$$

where $m_{c \to i}$ denotes the message sent from a node c to its neighbor node i. The final belief of node i is its downward belief which is the unnormalized marginal, i.e. $\text{MI}(\varphi) = \int_\mathbb{R} [\![x_i \models \varphi_i]\!] \cdot b_i(x_i) \, dx_i$.

Notice that even though the integration is symbolically defined over the whole real domain, the SMT-$\mathcal{LRA}$ logical constraints in formulas $\varphi_{i,j}$ and φ_i would give integration bounds that are linear in the variables. This guarantees that our messages will be univariate piecewise polynomials.

Proposition 5. Let φ be an SMT-$\mathcal{LRA}$ formula with tree primal graph, then the messages as defined in Equation 5.8 and beliefs as defined in Equation 5.9 are univariate piecewise polynomials.

Remark 5. The multiplication of two piecewise polynomial functions $f_1(x)$ and $f_2(x)$ is defined as a piecewise polynomial function $f(x)$ whose domain is the intersection of the domains of these two functions and for each x in its domain, the value is defined as $f(x) = f_1(x) \cdot f_2(x)$.

In figure 5.3 we show an example of the two passes in MP-MI and we summarize the whole MP-MI scheme in Algorithm 2. There, two functions *critical-points* and *symbolic-bounds* are subroutines used to compute the numeric and symbolic bounds of integration for our pieces of univariate polynomials. Both of them can be efficiently implemented, see [109] for details. Concerning the actual integration of the polynomial pieces, this can be done efficiently symbolically, a task supported by many scientific computing packages. Next we will show how the beliefs and messages obtained from MP-MI can be leveraged for inference tasks.

Algorithm 2 MP-MI(φ) – Message Passing Model Integration

1: $\mathbf{V}_{\text{up}} \leftarrow$ sort nodes in $\mathcal{G}_\varphi$, children before parents
2: **for each** $X_i \in \mathbf{V}_{\text{up}}$ **do** send-message($X_i, X_{\text{parent}(X)}$)
$\qquad\qquad\qquad\qquad\qquad\qquad\qquad\qquad\qquad\qquad\qquad$ ▷ upward pass

3: $\mathbf{V}_{\text{down}} \leftarrow$ sort nodes in $\mathcal{G}_\varphi$, parents before children
4: **for each** $X_i \in \mathbf{V}_{\text{down}}$ **do** $\qquad\qquad\qquad\qquad\qquad\qquad$ ▷ downward pass
5: $\qquad$ **for each** $X_c \in \text{ch}(X_i)$ **do** send-message(X_i, X_c)
6: **Return** $\{\mathsf{b}_i\}_{i:X\in\mathcal{G}}$

send-message(X_i, X_j)

1: $\mathsf{b}_i \leftarrow$ compute-beliefs $\qquad\qquad\qquad\qquad\qquad\qquad\qquad\qquad$ ▷ cf. Equation 5.9
2: $P \leftarrow$ critical-points($\mathsf{b}_i, \varphi_i, \varphi_{i,j}$), $\quad I \leftarrow$ intervals-from-points(P) $\qquad$ ▷ cf. SMI in [109]
3: **for** interval $[l, u] \in I$ consistent with formula $\varphi_i \wedge \varphi_{i,j}$ **do**
4: $\qquad \langle l_s, u_s, f \rangle \leftarrow$ symbolic-bounds($\mathsf{b}_i, [l, u], \varphi_{i,j}$)
5: $\qquad f' \leftarrow \int_l^u f(x_i)\, dx_i, \quad \mathsf{m}_{i\to j} \leftarrow \mathsf{m}_{i\to j} \cup \langle l, u, f' \rangle$
6: **Return** $\mathsf{m}_{i\to j}$

5.3.2 Amortizing Queries

Given a SMT-$\mathcal{LRA}$ formula φ, in the next Propositions, we show that we can leverage beliefs and messages computed by MP-MI to speed up (amortize) inference time over multiple queries on formula φ. More specifically, when given queries that conform to the structure of formula φ, i.e. queries on a node variable or queries over variables that are connected by an edge in graph $\mathcal{G}_\varphi$, we can reuse the local information encoded in beliefs.

Expectations and moments can also be computed efficiently by leveraging beliefs and taking ratios. They are pivotal in several scenarios including inference and learning.

Proposition 6. Let φ be an SMT-$\mathcal{LRA}$ formula with a tree primal graph, and let Φ be an SMT-$\mathcal{LRA}$ query over variable $X_i \in \mathbf{X}$. It holds that $\text{MI}(\varphi \wedge \Phi) = \int_\mathbb{R} [\![x_i \models \Phi]\!] [\![x_i \models \varphi_i]\!] \mathsf{b}_i(x_i) dx_i$.

Proposition 7. Let φ be an SMT-$\mathcal{LRA}$ formula and let Φ be an SMT-$\mathcal{LRA}$ query over $X_i, X_j \in \mathbf{X}$ that are connected in tree primal graph $\mathcal{G}_\varphi$. The updated message from node j to node i is as follows.

$$\mathsf{m}^*_{j\to i}(x_i) = \int_\mathbb{R} \mathsf{b}_j(x_j)/\mathsf{m}_{i\to j}(x_j) \times [\![x_i, x_j \models \varphi_{i,j} \wedge \Phi]\!][\![x_j \models \varphi_j]\!]\, dx_j$$

It holds that $\text{MI}(\varphi \wedge \Phi) = \int_\mathbb{R} [\![x_i \models \varphi_i]\!] \cdot \mathsf{b}^*_i(x_i) dx_i$ with b^*_i obtained from the updated message $\mathsf{m}^*_{j\to i}$.

Proposition 8. Let φ be an SMT-$\mathcal{LRA}$ formula with tree primal graph, then the k-th moment of variable $X_i \in \mathbf{X}$ can be obtained by $\mathbb{E}[X_i^k] = \frac{1}{\text{MI}(\varphi)} \int_\mathbb{R} [\![x_i \models \varphi_i]\!] \times x_i^k \mathsf{b}_i(x_i)\, dx_i$.

Pre-computing beliefs and messages can dramatically speed up inference by amortization, as we will show in section 5.4.

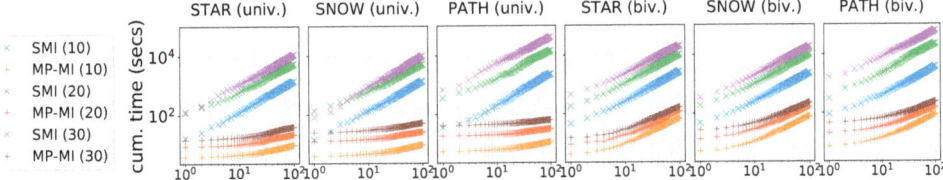

Figure 5.4: Log-log plot of cumulative time (seconds, y-axis) for MP-MI (orange, red) and SMI (blue, green) over STAR, SNOW and PATH primal graphs (see text) with 10, 20 and 30 variables for 100 univariate and bivariate queries (x-axis).

This is especially important when the primal graphs have large diameter. In fact, recall from section 5.2 that even when the formula φ has a tree-shaped primal graph, but unbounded diameter, computing MI is still hard.

5.3.3 Complexity of MP-MI

As we mention in our analysis on the inherent hardness of MI problems in section 5.2, our proposed MP-MI scheme runs efficiently on MI problems with tree-shaped and balanced tree primal graphs. Here we formally derive its algorithmic complexity. To do so, we leverage the concept of a pseudo tree. The pseudo tree is a directed tree with the shortest diameter among all the spanning trees of an undirected primal graph. In MP-MI this is equivalent to select a root r in the primal graph such that it is the root of the pseudo tree and its child-parent relationships guide the execution of the upward and downward passes.

Theorem 4. Consider an SMT-$\mathcal{LRA}$ formula φ with a tree primal graph with diameter h_p, and a pseudo tree with l leaves and diameter h_t. Let m be the number of literals in formula φ, and n be the number of variables. Then MI (φ) can be computed in $O(l \cdot (n^3 \cdot m^h)^h)$ by the MP-MI algorithm.

This result comes from the fact that, when choosing the same node as root, the *upward pass* of MP-MI essentially corresponds to the SMI algorithm in [109] when symbolic integration is applied. While SMI can only compute the unnormalized marginal of the root node, MP-MI can obtain all unnormalized marginals for all nodes. Therefore, the complexity of MP-MI is linear in the complexity of one run of SMI. Based on the complexity results in Theorem 4, MP-MI is potentially exponential in the diameter of $\mathcal{G}_\varphi$. Note that this results from the fact that the size of a single message, i.e. the number of pieces in its piecewise polynomial representation (cf. Eq. 5.8), is not bounded by the treewidth of primal graph $\mathcal{G}_\varphi$ but increases exponentially in the diameter of $\mathcal{G}_\varphi$.

This, together with the fact that belief propagation is polynomial for discrete domains with tree primal graphs, indicates that performing inference over hybrid or continuous domains with logical constrains in SMT-$\mathcal{LRA}$ is inherently more difficult than that in discrete domains. The increase in complexity from discrete domains to continuous domains is not simply a matter of our inability to find good algorithms but the inherent hardness of the problem.

5.4 Experiments

In this section, we present a preliminary empirical evaluation to answer the following research questions: i) how does our MP-MI compare with SMI, the search-based approach to MI [109]? ii) how beneficial is amortizing multiple queries with MP-MI? We implemented MP-MI in Python 3, using the scientific computing python package *sympy* for symbolic integration, the *MathSAT5* SMT solver [19] and the *pysmt* package [34] for manipulating and representing SMT-$\mathcal{LRA}$ formulas.

We compare MP-MI with SMI on synthetic SMT-$\mathcal{LRA}$ formulas over $n \in \{10, 20, 30\}$ variables and comprising both univariate and bivariate literals. In order to investigate the effect of adopting tree primal graphs with different diameters we considered: star-shaped graphs (STAR) with diameters two and complete ternary trees (SNOW) with diameters being $\log(n)$ and linear chains (PATH) with diameters of length n. These synthetic structures were originally investigated by the authors of SMI and are prototypical tree structures that can be encountered in the real world while being easy to interpret due to their regularity.

Figure 5.4 shows the cumulative runtime of random queries that involve both univariate and bivariate literals. As expected, MP-MI takes a fraction time than SMI (up to two order of magnitudes) to answer 100 univariate or bivariate queries in all experimental scenarios, since it is able to amortize inference *inter-query*. More surprisingly, MP-MI is even faster than SMI to compute a single query. This is due to the fact that SMI solves polynomial integration numerically, by first reconstructing the univariate polynomials using interpolation e.g. Lagrange interpolation, while in MP-MI we adopt symbolical integration. Hence the complexity of the former is always quadratic in the degree of the polynomial, while for the latter the average case is linear in the number of monomials in the polynomial to integrate, which in practice might be much less than the degree of the polynomial.

5.5 Final remarks

The theoretical analysis presented in section 5.2 led to the development of MP-MI, the first efficient algorithm for tractable MI problems. This work is quite preliminary, in fact, an extended version that generalizes our findings to the weighted case is currently under review.

The requirements for tractability in MI are quite restrictive and the problems considered in the empirical evaluation presented in section 5.4 are not prototypical of those that can usually arise from real world applications. Nonetheless, these advancements pave the way to the development of approximate algorithms that work in more general settings.

A direction that we are currently exploring follows the ideas of Relax-Compensate-Recover (RCR) [17], an anytime inference framework that works by relaxing the dependencies of an intractable problem until tractability is achieved. An exact algorithm is then used to perform inference in the tractable, relaxed model. This framework accounts for the relaxed dependencies by introducing additional variables and potentials in the relaxed, tractable model and matching their moments (or marginals) accordingly. Thus, the ability of MP-MI of computing the marginals and moments efficiently is pivotal.

A natural question is whether the message passing scheme presented in section 5.3 can be generalized to n-dimensional messages, leading to a jointree-like algorithm [62, 43, 97] for WMI. This interesting research direction is left for future work.

CHAPTER 6

LARIAT

6.1 Learning WMI distributions

We are concerned with learning WMI distributions, that is, hybrid distributions with a structured support. Formally, our learning problem can be stated as follows:

Definition 10 (WMI learning). Given a dataset $\mathcal{D}$ of feasible samples drawn i.i.d. from an unknown hybrid structured distribution P^* with true support χ^*, find a WMI distribution $\langle \hat{w}, \hat{\chi} \rangle$ that well approximates P^*.

Notice that P^* is not required to be a WMI distribution, and that χ^* is not required to be an SMT formula. In principle this is not an issue, because (complex enough) WMI distributions can approximate any hybrid structured distribution.

We are now ready to introduce our approach, LARIAT (for LeARning to IntegrATe). Let $\mathcal{D} = \{(\mathbf{x}^s, \mathbf{a}^s)\}_{s=1}^{S}$ be the samples at our disposal, where $\mathbf{x}^s$ and $\mathbf{a}^s$ are the values assigned to $\mathbf{X}$ and $\mathbf{A}$, respectively. LARIAT estimates a WMI distribution from $\mathcal{D}$ by breaking the learning problem into two tasks: 1) learning a support $\hat{\chi}$; and 2) learning a weight function $\hat{w}$ compatible with $\hat{\chi}$. The first step is handled by a novel generalization of INCAL [52], a state-of-the-art method for learning SMT formulas. The second step uses a hybrid density estimator to learn a weight function. Finally, LARIAT normalizes the latter to trim away the unfeasible areas. We discuss these steps in detail.

6.1.1 Learning the support

Given examples of positive (feasible) and negative (infeasible) variable assignments, INCAL learns an SMT formula φ that covers all positive and no negative examples. Support learning can be reduced to a similar problem, namely finding a formula $\hat{\chi}$ that generalizes from the feasible samples $\mathcal{D}$ to their underlying true support χ^*. Here we briefly overview INCAL, and then introduce INCAL+, our generalization of the former to support learning.

Learning SMT formulas with INCAL   Given a set $\mathcal{D}$ of positive and negative examples and a maximum number of clauses k and unique linear inequalities h, INCAL finds a CNF (or DNF) formula φ of the given complexity that correctly classifies all examples. The search is encoded as an SMT-$\mathcal{LRA}$ satisfaction problem and solved with an SMT solver, e.g., MathSAT [19] or Z3 [24]; the full SMT encoding can be found in [52]. This non-greedy learning strategy can acquire SMT formulas with non-convex feasible sets and oblique $\mathcal{LRA}$ atoms, which lie at the core of WMI distributions and are beyond the reach of greedier approaches (see [52] for a discussion).

INCAL employs an incremental scheme whereby a candidate formula is gradually adapted to correctly classify progressively larger subsets of the data. At iteration i, a formula φ_i that correctly classifies a subset $\mathcal{D}_i$ of the data is computed. Next, some of the examples $\mathcal{V}_i \subseteq \mathcal{D} \setminus \mathcal{D}_i$ inconsistent with φ_i are added to $\mathcal{D}_i$ to obtain $\mathcal{D}_{i+1}$ and the process repeats. Empirically, this allows learning a formula by encoding a small fraction of the dataset, with noticeable runtime benefits.

If the target formula complexity (k, h) is not given, INCAL automatically searches for a formula of minimal complexity that covers all positive and no negative examples. This is achieved by gradually increasing k and h (initially set to 1 and 0, respectively) until an appropriate formula is found.

Learning supports with INCAL+   We cast support learning as the problem of finding an SMT formula $\hat{\chi}$ that covers all of the positive examples and does not cover regions too "far away" from them, as determined by some distance measure d over $\mathbf{X} \times \mathbf{A}$ and a user-provided threshold $\theta > 0$ over it.

More specifically, let $\mathcal{B}_\theta$ be the union of S bounding boxes, each of size θ, centered around the samples in $\mathcal{D}$:

$$\mathcal{B}_\theta := \bigcup_{s=1}^{S} \{ (\mathbf{x}, \mathbf{a}) \mid d((\mathbf{x}^s, \mathbf{a}^s), (\mathbf{x}, \mathbf{a})) \leq \theta \}$$

Also, let $\bar{\mathcal{B}}_\theta$ be its complement. Our assumption is that θ can be chosen so that $\mathcal{B}_\theta$ is a reasonably tight overapproximation of the true support χ^*. In this case, if $\hat{\chi}$ approximates $\mathcal{B}_\theta$ and does not cover any of $\bar{\mathcal{B}}_\theta$, then it will also be a good approximation of the true support. (The algorithm can be trivially adapted to allow for $\mathcal{B}_\theta$ to be an underapproximation instead.) Since too complex supports (in terms of k and h) can overfit, we wish to minimize complexity.

This leads to the INCAL+ support learning problem:

$$\min_{\hat{\chi}} \ k + h$$

$$\text{s.t. } (\mathbf{x}^s, \mathbf{a}^s) \models \hat{\chi} \qquad\qquad \forall (\mathbf{x}^s, \mathbf{a}^s) \in \mathcal{D} \qquad\qquad (6.1)$$

$$(\mathbf{x}^-, \mathbf{a}^-) \not\models \hat{\chi} \qquad\qquad \forall (\mathbf{x}^-, \mathbf{a}^-) \in \bar{\mathcal{B}}_\theta \qquad\qquad (6.2)$$

where $s = 1, \ldots, S$ ranges over all samples in the dataset. As underlying distance we choose $d((\mathbf{x}, \mathbf{a}), (\mathbf{x}', \mathbf{a}')) = \mathsf{ite}(\mathbf{a} = \mathbf{a}', \max_i(x_i - x_i'), \infty)$, which admits an SMT-$\mathcal{LRA}$ representation.

This formulation can not be solved directly, because of the universal quantifier in Eq. 6.2.

Algorithm 3 The inner loop of the INCAL+ algorithm. FINDFORMULA uses the INCAL encoding to look for an SMT formula of complexity at most (k, h) that correctly classifies $\mathcal{D}_i$.

1: **procedure** LEARN($\mathcal{D}$: samples, (k, h): complexity)
2:     $\mathcal{V}_0 \leftarrow \mathcal{D}_1 \leftarrow$ sample from $\mathcal{D}$, $i \leftarrow 1$
3:     **while** $|\mathcal{V}_{i-1}| > 0$ **do**
4:         $\hat{\chi}_i \leftarrow$ FINDFORMULA($\mathcal{D}_i, k, h$)
5:         **if** the solver returns unsat **then**
6:             **return** no support
7:         $\mathcal{V}_i \leftarrow$ all misclassified samples in $\mathcal{D} \setminus \mathcal{D}_i$
8:         **if** $\mathcal{V}_i \neq \varnothing$ **then**
9:             $\mathcal{V}_i \leftarrow$ sample from $\mathcal{V}_i$
10:        **else**
11:            $\mathcal{V}_i \leftarrow$ a wrongly covered sample in $\bar{\mathcal{B}}_\theta$
12:        $\mathcal{D}_{i+1} \leftarrow \mathcal{D}_i \cup \mathcal{V}_i$, $i \leftarrow i + 1$
13:    **return** $\hat{\chi}_i$

• Pos. example   ◦ Neg. example   ⬚ Pos. bounding box

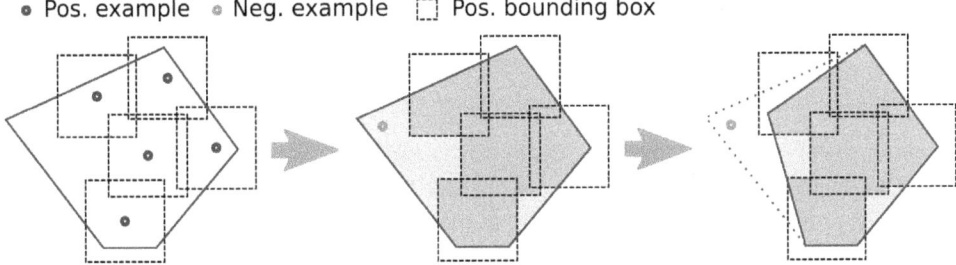

Figure 6.1: A depiction of the iterative INCAL+ procedure, with the blue solid line representing the current support $\hat{\chi}_i$. Left: bounding box construction around $\mathcal{D}_i$. Center: a negative example is sampled from $\bar{\mathcal{B}}_\theta \wedge \neg \hat{\chi}_i$. Right: the support $\hat{\chi}_{i+1}$ accounts for the negative example.

For given (k, h), we solve it with INCAL, by exploiting its incremental learning scheme (see Algorithm 3). First, an initial subset $\mathcal{D}_1$ is obtained (at line 2) by sampling examples from $\mathcal{D}$. Then, at each iteration i, INCAL+ computes a formula φ_i that correctly classifies $\mathcal{D}_i \subseteq \mathcal{D}$ (line 4), and a set misclassified variable assignments $\mathcal{V}_i$ is obtained from $\mathcal{D}$; if none are found, a new, misclassified negative is taken from $\bar{\mathcal{B}}_\theta \wedge \neg \hat{\chi}_i$ (lines 7–11). Finding a negative example $(\mathbf{x}^-, \mathbf{a}^-) \in \bar{\mathcal{B}}_\theta$ that is wrongly covered by $\hat{\chi}_i$ (line 11) is done via SMT by solving:

$$\hat{\chi}_i \quad \wedge \quad \bigwedge_s (d((\mathbf{x}^s, \mathbf{a}^s), (\mathbf{x}^-, \mathbf{a}^-)) > \theta) \quad \wedge \quad \text{BK}$$

where s iterates over the examples in $\mathcal{D}$ and BK is background knowledge that should not be relearned, such as mutual exclusivity of Boolean variables used as a one-hot encoding of discrete multi-valued attributes.

The violating examples are then added to $\mathcal{D}_i$ to obtain $\mathcal{D}_{i+1}$ and the loop repeats. This process is depicted in figure 6.1. INCAL+ stops when no violating examples can be found. To improve

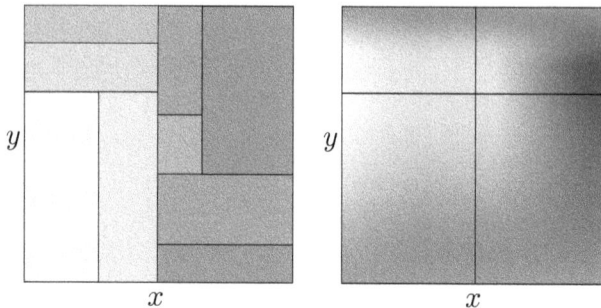

Figure 6.2: Left: an illustrative bivariate density modelled by a DET as a piecewise constant function. constant density function encoded by a DET. Right: the same density modelled by a MSPN with mixtures of univariate linear functions for x (in blue) and y (in red).

the runtime of the algorithm, initial negative examples sampled from $\bar{\mathcal{B}}_\theta$ (e.g., through rejection sampling) can be added to the initial dataset.

Like the original algorithm, if the target complexity (k, h) is not known, the above procedure can be wrapped into a loop that gradually increases k and h whenever an appropriate formula can not be found (line 6). This is guaranteed to converge to a correct formula, if one exists [52].

To automatically select a viable threshold θ, we dynamically explore various thresholds $\theta_i = m_i \cdot \theta_{nn}$, where θ_{nn} is the average closest distance between neighbors in $\mathcal{D}$. Since smaller thresholds provide more detailed supports but increase the runtime, we use an exponential-search based procedure to quickly find the smallest multiple m_i for which INCAL+ can learn a support within a given time budget t. Starting with an initial multiplier m_1 and given a maximal number of steps N, at each step we run INCAL+ with threshold θ_i for at most t seconds, increasing the multiplier if a support was found, and decreasing it when INCAL+ timed out.

6.1.2 Learning the weight function

Since the weight function w behaves like a structured density function, it can in principle be estimated by any hybrid density estimation technique. We focus on two state-of-the-art models, Density Estimation Trees (DETs) and Mixed Sum-Product Networks (MSPNs), which we introduce next. A major limitation is that these estimators can not learn nor model oblique structured supports. Below we show how LARIAT lifts this limitation by *normalizing* the estimated densities with respect to a learned SMT-$\mathcal{LRA}$ support.

Density Estimation Trees DETs are a density estimation analogue of standard decision trees. The internal nodes recursively partition the space with univariate, axis-aligned $\mathcal{LRA}$ conditions (aka *splits*), while the leaves define uniform density functions, as shown in figure 6.2 (left). DETs are learned from data using an iterative procedure, whereby splits are introduced so as to greedily optimize (a surrogate of) the integrated square error [86]. The procedure terminates when a pre-specified minimal number of instances is covered by each leaf. In order to control overfitting, the resulting tree is then pruned. The whole learning procedure allows piecewise constant densities to be efficiently learned from data.

DETs have a number of useful features. First, under suitable conditions, DETs are provably consistent [86]. Just like decision trees can approximate any Boolean function, deep enough DETs can approximate any weight function to arbitrary precision. Second, given a DET, the weighted model integral of any axis-aligned query φ can be easily computed by partitioning φ according to the leaves and summing the resulting integrals.

DETs also have limitations. The shallow DETs that are used in practice can not approximate oblique $\mathcal{LRA}$ supports. Moreover, DET leaves have constant density and may fail to accurately represent non-constant densities. Finally, since leaves always contain at least one example, DETs can only model trivial supports [86].

Mixed Sum-Product Networks   Mixed Sum-Product Networks (MSPNs) [72] are state-of-the-art models for hybrid domains. MSPNs extend Sum-Product Networks [84] by introducing continuous variables and densities. They encode a circuit where the leaves define piecewise polynomial distributions over the input variables, and the internal nodes are sums (i.e., mixtures) or products of their child nodes, as depicted in figure 6.2 (right).

Like DETs, MSPNs are learned greedily from data. The learning algorithm recursively splits the dataset by either: i) partitioning the input variables into independent sets, which amounts to introducing a product node, or ii) clustering similar examples together, thus introducing a sum node. If no split can be found (e.g., if there's only one example/variable in the current dataset), a polynomial leaf node is fit on the data. In practice, MSPNs implementations support univariate constant or linear leaves only.

By exploiting context-specific independencies, MSPNs can be much more compact than DETs, while still allowing for tractable inference of marginal and conditional queries. Indeed, if the queried quantity decomposes over the circuit, then inference amounts to a couple of bottom-up evaluations.

6.1.3   Normalization

The third and final step of LARIAT is *normalization*. Given a support $\hat{\chi}$ and a learned piecewise polynomial weight function $\tilde{w}$, normalization aims at redistributing the density of $\tilde{w}$ away from the unfeasible region outside of $\hat{\chi}$ and inside the feasible one. After normalization, the resulting weight function $\hat{w}$ has to satisfy the properties: p_1) $\mathsf{WMI}(\neg\hat{\chi}, \hat{w}) = 0$; and p_2) $\mathsf{WMI}(\hat{\chi}, \hat{w}) = 1$.

Global normalization   These two properties give rise to a simple, yet effective normalization scheme which defines:

$$\hat{w} = \mathsf{ite}(\hat{\chi}, \frac{\tilde{w}}{\mathsf{WMI}(\hat{\chi}, \tilde{w})}, 0)$$

As depicted in figure 6.3 (right), the density falling outside $\hat{\chi}$ is distributed uniformly in the resulting model.

It is trivial to see that properties p_1 and p_2 are satisfied, however, to improve the likelihood of the resulting density, we can resort to a more elaborate normalization scheme.

Local Normalization   Local density estimators, like DETs, partition the space into sub-regions defined by mutually exclusive SMT formulas χ_i and fit a local density $\tilde{w}_i$ for every sub-region i. The idea behind local normalization is to retain the space partitioning induced by the learner but to (locally) normalize the densities within every subregion such that: $\mathsf{WMI}(\chi_i \wedge \neg\hat{\chi}, \hat{w}_i) = 0$ and $\mathsf{WMI}(\chi_i \wedge \hat{\chi}, \hat{w}_i) = \mathsf{WMI}(\chi_i, \tilde{w}_i)$, where $\hat{w}_i$ is the normalized local density. This normalization scheme is depicted in figure 6.3 (center). It follows that, since the χ_i exhaustively partition the entire space and $\mathsf{WMI}(\top, \tilde{w}) = 1$, the properties p_1 and p_2 are both satisfied. The local normalized density $\hat{w}_i$ can be computed as:

$$\text{norm}^* : \hat{w}_i = \tilde{w}_i \cdot \mathsf{WMI}(\chi_i, \tilde{w}_i) / \mathsf{WMI}(\chi_i \wedge \hat{\chi}, \tilde{w}_i)$$
$$\text{norm}^+ : \hat{w}_i = \tilde{w}_i + \mathsf{WMI}(\chi_i \wedge \neg\hat{\chi}, \tilde{w}_i) / \text{vol}(\chi_i \wedge \hat{\chi})$$

Local normalization for DETs   In the case of DETs, local densities $\tilde{w}_i$ are computed as $\tilde{w}_i = \frac{1}{S}\frac{S}{\text{vol}(\chi)}$, and we obtain, using $S = |\mathcal{D}|$ for the total number of samples and $S_i = |\mathcal{D} \models \chi_i|$ for the number of samples that satisfy χ_i:

$$\hat{w}_i = \frac{1}{S}\frac{S_i}{\text{vol}(\chi_i)} \cdot \frac{\mathsf{WMI}(\chi_i, \tilde{w}_i)}{\mathsf{WMI}(\chi_i \wedge \hat{\chi}, \tilde{w}_i)} = \frac{1}{S}\frac{S_i}{\text{vol}(\chi_i \wedge \hat{\chi})}.$$

There are three properties of DETs which makes local normalization especially attractive: 1) DETs explicitly describe the sub-regions; 2) norm* and norm+ yield the same result since $\tilde{w}_i$ is constant; and 3) since every DET subregion contains at least one sample, no subregion can become entirely infeasible. Local normalization is computationally more expensive than global normalization, however, for locally fit models (like DETs) it obtains more accurate models.

Example 20. Consider a learned weight function (DET) consisting of two non-zero subregions whose local densities have been fitted based on the number of samples in those sub-regions ($\frac{1}{4}$th of the samples in the first, and $\frac{3}{4}$th of the samples in the second sub-region):

$$\tilde{w} = \begin{cases} 0.25 & \text{if } (0 \leq x \leq 1) \wedge (0 \leq y \leq 1) \\ 0.75 & \text{if } (0 \leq x \leq 1) \wedge (1 < y \leq 2) \end{cases}$$

and a support $\hat{\chi} = (y \geq x)$. The support only cuts away feasible volume from the first sub-region, meaning that the samples falling into the first sub-region are now distributed over a smaller volume. Therefore, the local normalization procedure increases the density over the remaining feasible volume in the first sub-region, while leaving the second sub-region untouched. We obtain the normalized weight function:

$$\hat{w} = \begin{cases} 0.5 & \text{if } (0 \leq x \leq 1) \wedge (0 \leq y \leq 1) \wedge (y \geq x) \\ 0.75 & \text{if } (0 \leq x \leq 1) \wedge (1 < y \leq 2) \end{cases}$$

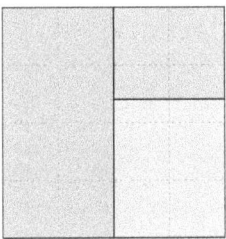 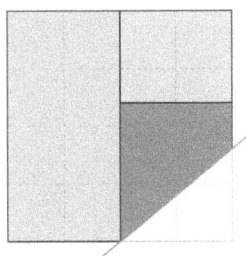 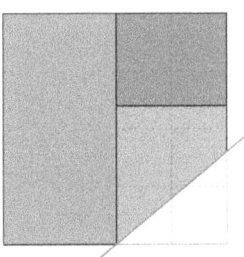

Figure 6.3: Graphical representation of the proposed normalization schemes. Left: the original piecewise constant density $\tilde{w}$. Center: the effect of the local normalization. Right: the effect of the global normalization.

Local normalization for generic densities   First, to normalize generic weight functions encoded as ASTs (e.g., MSPNs) which only indirectly describe the sub-regions and their densities, we can compile the ASTs into equivalent XADDs [50] that support the enumeration of sub-regions and integration. Second, the choice between norm* and norm+ is left up to the user. Third, the density of completely infeasible sub-regions is redistributed over the entire feasible space akin to global normalization. It is important to note that normalization of models like MSPNs that support tractable inference generally may render inference intractable.

Both normalization schemes are amenable to any support, be it learned with INCAL+ or provided by a domain expert (as can be the case in security applications). Since they can can deal with arbitrary WMI distributions, other density estimators such as MARS (see Related Work), can also be readily converted to WMI and normalized.

6.2   Experiments

In this section, we explore the following research questions[1]: **Q1**) Does INCAL+ learn reasonable supports? **Q2**) Does LARIAT improve over state-of-the-art density estimators when the true support is provided? **Q3**) Does LARIAT improve over state-of-the-art density estimators when the support is estimated by INCAL+? We address the first two questions on synthetic datasets of increasing complexity, and the last one on both synthetic and real-world datasets.

Each synthetic dataset was obtained by first generating a random WMI distribution $\langle \chi^*, w^* \rangle$ with a given number of Boolean b and continuous variables r, and then sampling examples (i.e. feasible configurations) from it. More specifically: i) w^* was a random XADD sampled by recursively adding internal and leaf nodes up to a fixed depth $d = 2$, where the internal nodes partition the space with a random SMT-$\mathcal{LRA}$ formula, while the leaves host a randomly generated non-negative polynomial of maximum degree $2r$. ii) χ^* was obtained by sampling a CNF formula with h hyperplanes and l literals using the procedure of [52]. Without loss of generality, we restricted the range of the continuous variables to $[0, 1]$.

---

[1]The code is available at: `https://github.com/weighted-model-integration/LARIAT`

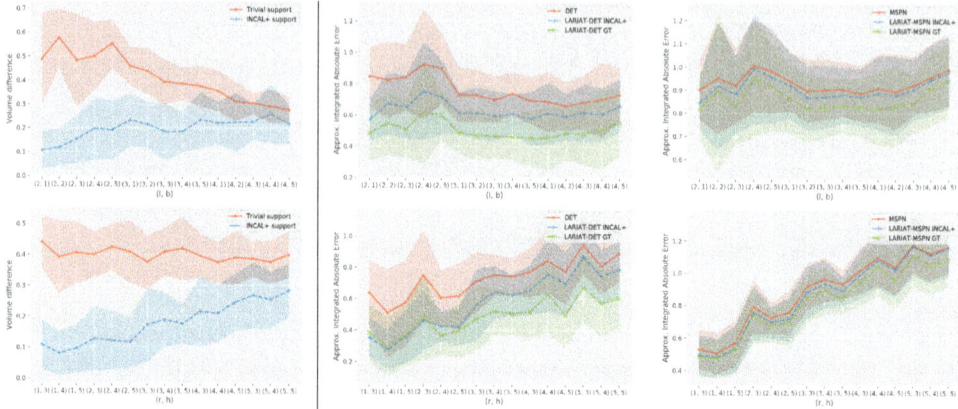

Figure 6.4: Results on the synthetic datasets. Left: volume of the difference of the true support and the learned (blue) or trivial (red) ones for varying $\langle l, b \rangle$ (top) and $\langle r, h \rangle$ (bottom). Middle: IAE of DETs (red) vs. LARIAT-DETs with learned (blue) and ground truth (green) support. Right: IAE of MSPNs (red) vs. LARIAT-MSPNs with learned (blue) and ground truth (green) support. (Best viewed in color.)

We evaluated how the complexity of the true distribution impacts the performance of INCAL+ and LARIAT by generating increasingly complex supports, either by fixing $b = 3, l = 3$ and varying h and r, or by fixing $r = 3, h = 5$ and increasing l and b, for a total of 30 configurations. For each configuration, we generated 20 different ground-truth models and relative dataset, each consisting of 500 training and 50 validation examples.

Learning the support In order to answer **Q1**, we ran INCAL+ on the synthetic datasets, using a timeout of 300 seconds for each call, and measured the misclassification error between the true and the learned support, which amounts to the volume of the symmetric difference of the two supports, that is, $\text{vol}((\hat{\chi} \wedge \neg \chi^*) \vee (\neg \hat{\chi} \wedge \chi^*))$.

In these experiments we ran INCAL+ on training data $\mathcal{D}_{\mathcal{T}}$ and used the validation data $\mathcal{D}_{\mathcal{V}}$ to select the learned support that minimizes:

$$\frac{\text{vol}(\chi \wedge \neg \mathcal{B}'_\theta)}{\text{vol}(\neg \mathcal{B}'_\theta)} + \frac{\sum_{(\mathbf{x}, \mathbf{a}) \in \mathcal{D}} \mathbb{1}((\mathbf{x}^s, \mathbf{a}^s) \models \chi)}{|\mathcal{D}_{\mathcal{V}}|}$$

where $\mathbb{1}(\ldots)$ is the indicator function and $\mathcal{B}'_\theta$ is the formula that encodes the union of bounding boxes of size θ around the points in $\mathcal{D}_{\mathcal{V}}$, being θ the threshold used to learn χ. Figure 6.4 (left) shows the average and standard deviation misclassification error (normalized in $[0, 1]$) for each set of parameters. INCAL+ is compared to the trivial support, given by the range of each single variable in the dataset. Results show that INCAL+ learns a support that substantially improves on the trivial one in all settings, apart for a few instances for $l = 4$ where it timed out. This allows us to answer question **Q1** affirmatively.

Learning synthetic distributions   We addressed **Q2** and **Q3** by comparing the distribution learned by the density estimator alone (DET or MSPN) with the one learned by LARIAT using ground truth **(Q2)** and INCAL+ estimated **(Q3)** support.

Contrary to the previous support learning experiment, INCAL+ was run on $\mathcal{D}_T \cup \mathcal{D}_V$. Weight learning was performed on $\mathcal{D}_T$ only, reserving the validation set $\mathcal{D}_V$ to select the best support among those learned by INCAL+, as the one yielding the highest log-likelihood on $\mathcal{D}_V$. For DETs, the validation set was also used to prune the tree.

We measured the quality of the learned distributions $\langle \hat{\chi}, \hat{w} \rangle$ by measuring the integrated absolute error (IAE) with respect to the true distribution:

$$\mathsf{IAE}(\hat{w}, w^*) = \sum_{\mathbf{A}} \int_{\hat{\chi} \vee \chi} |\hat{w}(\mathbf{X}, \mathbf{A}) - w^*(\mathbf{X}, \mathbf{A})| \, d\mathbf{X}$$

Since computing the exact value of IAE is computationally prohibitive, we performed a Monte Carlo approximation with 1,000,000 samples drawn from the ground truth distribution using rejection sampling with a uniform proposal.

The average IAEs and their standard deviations are shown in figure 6.4 (middle) and (right) when using DET and MSPN estimators respectively. The results affirmatively answer **Q2**, as LARIAT with ground truth support achieves substantial improvements over the density estimators alone, for both DET and MSPN. The same holds for **Q3** when using a DET estimator, even if the improvements are clearly more limited. Conversely, the supports learned appear not as effective when applied to the global normalization.

Learning real-world distributions   In order to check whether the improvements shown by LARIAT in the synthetic experiments hold in real world scenarios, we tested its performance on real-world datasets (question **Q3**). The categorical features found in the data were converted to (sets of) Boolean variables via *one-hot-encoding*. The resulting mutual exclusivity constraints were used to initialize both INCAL+ and the sampling procedures. Support and weight learning were run using the same setting used for the synthetic distributions.

We evaluated LARIAT on the hybrid UCI benchmarks contained in the MLC++ library, which includes 18 hybrid datasets from different real-world domains. On some datasets, INCAL+ was not able to discover any non-trivial support on the full hybrid space before timing out. In those cases, the search was then performed on the numerical subspace, allowing INCAL+ to learn linear relationships among the continuous variables. Table 6.1 shows the average log-likelihood computed on the test set for each dataset. Notice that the log-likelihood of test points falling outside the model support is $-\infty$. In order to apply the metric in our structured and hybrid spaces, we follow the approach of [72] and substitute each $\log(0)$ in the average with a large negative constant. Also, it is worth mentioning that in continuous (sub)spaces the value of the average log-likelihood is not necessarily non-positive, as it is in fact computed on the probability density function.

For the most complex tasks, LARIAT-DET is sometimes unable to complete the local normalization within reasonable time. If the local normalization timeout (set to $1200s$) is reached,

Dataset	DET	+LARIAT	MSPN	+LARIAT
anneal-U	−61.2	**−38.5**	−41.9	**6.0**
australian	−44.1	**−30.1**	−32.8	**−27.8**
auto	−80.8	**−63.5**	−67.2	**−58.5**
balance-scale	−7.2	**−6.4**	−7.5	**−6.4**
breast	−29.6	**−29.2**	−26.1	**−25.2**
breast-cancer	−11.8	**−9.1**	−11.5	**−8.6**
cars	−40.1	**−29.5**	−29.2	**−26.8**
cleve	−31.2	**−26.9**	−28.0	**−25.8**
crx	−48.2	**−32.7**	−32.7	**−28.8**
diabetes	−28.8	**−27.9**	−30.3	**−29.4**
german	−46.1	**−36.4**	−39.4	**−33.3**
german-org	−28.8	**−28.6**	−27.5	**−25.2**
glass	−2.1	**1.6**	0.7	**3.7**
glass2	4.2	**4.8**	4.7	**5.2**
heart	−24.1	**−23.8**	−24.7	**−22.7**
hepatitis	−29.3	**−24.0**	−27.1	**−23.7**
iris	−4.3	**−3.4**	−2.9	**−2.7**
solar	−15.0	**−2.6**	−7.6	**3.3**

Table 6.1: Average log-likelihood on the test set for the UCI/MLC++ experiment. Bold text highlights a statistically significant improvement (p-value < 0.0001) in the test set log-likelihood of LARIAT over the unnormalized model.

LARIAT's fallback strategy is to apply the faster, global normalization.

Nevertheless, in every setting LARIAT improves the performance of the underlying model. We compared the log-likelihood of test set points using a Wilcoxon test, confirming that the improvement is significant for both DETs and MSPNs (p-value < 0.0001).

The tasks that benefited the most from LARIAT are characterized by a large amount of categorical and few continuous variables. A more extensive investigation of the factors contributing to the performance gains is left for future work.

6.3 Final remarks

This chapter described the first method that jointly learns the structure and weights of a WMI distribution from data. While the experiments in section 6.2 show that accounting for a structured oblique supports is generally beneficial, the approach of learning the support and weight separately is clearly not ideal. The oblique support can encode unfeasible regions of the space, but alone it can't fully represent all deterministic relationships between the variables. In fact, LARIAT-DETs and LARIAT-MSPNs retain the same internal structure of the density. Developing an unified framework for learning oblique densities and hard constraints is a relevant future direction.

Another aspect that was not considered in this preliminary work is performance of the learned model at inference time. Striking a balance between expressivity and tractability is crucial for the adoption of WMI in many complex real-world settings. Another interesting direction is thus learning tractable WMI models.

CHAPTER 7

CONCLUSION

This thesis presented my contributions to inference and learning in the context of WMI, which can be summarized as follows:

- WMI-PA improved over the existing solver-based approaches by accounting for the structure of the weight function. Taking into consideration the structural properties of the WMI problem is an effective idea that has been leveraged in different ways by more recent solvers. The performance gain brought by predicate abstraction also motivates further research in leveraging formal verification techniques in probabilistic inference algorithms. Prior work conceived WMI as a tool for answering probabilistic queries in hybrid graphical models. The alternative formulation that we proposed offers a different view and broadens the scope of WMI inference to hierarchical and circuit-based formalisms like DETs and MSPNs.

- Our work on MP-MI and the tractability boundaries of MI problems is not only foundational for its theoretical implications, but also suggests different research directions for improving the existing inference algorithms. On the one hand, this work characterizes WMI from a tractable modelling viewpoint. On the other hand, the message passing algorithm draws a parallel between WMI and extensively studied inference techniques in graphical models.

- Prior to our work, learning in WMI was an unexplored topic, with the exception of the maximum likelihood estimation of the parameters in the restricted case of piecewise constant potentials. LARIAT represents the first algorithm for learning both the structure and parameters of a WMI distribution directly from data. Accounting for a learned structured support has proven beneficial in many settings, which motivates the adoption of WMI as a modelling formalism and not only as a inference method.

WMI has attracted growing interest from the AI community and significant progress has been made during my PhD studies. Yet, there is room for improvement in many directions.

- Existing WMI-based inference techniques do not to scale to high dimensional domains with complex combinatorial structures. Promising directions include the hybridisation of SMT-based and symbolic techniques. Both approaches have their merits, with solver-based techniques being generally faster in the combinatorial aspect of reasoning and symbolic procedures being much more flexible and capable of exploiting structural properties of the problem that are out of reach of SMT solvers. Developing general and effective approximate algorithms is a crucial step for enabling WMI inference in large scale industrial problems. The existing approaches are either limited by distributional assumptions or struggle to provide practical error bounds. Another promising direction involves targeting inference in specific subclasses of WMI problems.

- Learning WMI representations from data is a novel and challenging field of research. Our work on LARIAT only scratched the surface of the problem and there is huge room for improvements in many aspects. Learning WMI models that guarantee efficient inference, such as tractable WMI models is currently an open problem. In LARIAT, the subtasks of learning the support and estimating the density are performed independently. A tighter integration between structure learning and parameter estimation would almost certainly be beneficial. This could be enabled by putting together ideas from MSPN learning, such as hybrid clustering, and hierarchical SMT learning. The existing work assumes a fully observed and noise-free setting. Investigating more challenging and realistic learning settings, such as those presented by noisy or missing observations is an open problem. Learning tractable WMI models such as mixtures of the models described in section 5.2 is another exciting but yet unexplored venue that could enable novel applications.

- Being a relatively novel field of study, much work has to be done in connecting the dots between different formalisms and approaches in hybrid structured models. While an approach for reducing inference in hybrid graphical models to WMI was initially proposed, investigating effective reduction algorithms and implementing them is a fundamental step toward bridging the gap between WMI-based inference algorithms and other techniques. In particular, recent work enabled MCMC techniques in highly complex piecewise distributions [3, 2, 4]. Adopting these approaches in the context of WMI is a promising direction.

- Promoting WMI-based techniques outside our research community and involving researchers from more applied fields is of primary importance. To this extent, pywmi is a first step towards making these techniques more accessible and foster the development of novel solvers. Releasing common benchmarks for comparing different techniques in hybrid structured domains is also an important goal. Although this research area is at its early stages, finding suitable real-world applications for WMI is a crucial line of research.

While AI has seen major breakthroughs in the last decades, many applications, such as safety-critical ones or those characterized by a high socio-economic impact, are currently out of reach of the existing techniques. While the current predictive models have shown remarkable performance in some tasks, aspects like robustness, verifiability and fairness are still considered open problems. AI has the potential of bringing huge benefits to humanity, although much work has to be done in developing trustable systems, characterized by high-level reasoning capabilities and transparent, verifiable behaviour. The study of hybrid logical/numerical reasoning in uncertain environments is a fundamental step towards this goal. My work on learning and reasoning in the context of WMI represents my modest contribution to the development of increasingly advanced hybrid structured probabilistic models. The proposed approaches pave the way to systems that will solve problems involving both numerical and logical aspects, possibly learning from observations how to deal with the uncertainty as well as the relational structure that characterize the task at hand. Thanks to their ability of both accounting for symbolic prior knowledge and answering complex and general queries, these techniques will enable an unprecedented level of control and transparency over the behaviour of our AI systems.

Bibliography

[1] Ralph Abboud, İsmail İlkan Ceylan, and Radoslav Dimitrov. "On the Approximability of Weighted Model Integration on DNF Structures". In: *Proceedings of the International Conference on Principles of Knowledge Representation and Reasoning*. Vol. 17. 1. 2020, pp. 828–837.

[2] Hadi Mohasel Afshar and Justin Domke. "Reflection, refraction, and hamiltonian monte carlo". In: *Advances in neural information processing systems*. 2015, pp. 3007–3015.

[3] Hadi Mohasel Afshar, Scott Sanner, and Ehsan Abbasnejad. "Linear-time gibbs sampling in piecewise graphical models". In: *Twenty-Ninth AAAI Conference on Artificial Intelligence*. 2015.

[4] Hadi Mohasel Afshar, Scott Sanner, and Christfried Webers. "Closed-Form Gibbs Sampling for Graphical Models with Algebraic Constraints." In: *AAAI*. 2016.

[5] Fahiem Bacchus, Shannon Dalmao, and Toniann Pitassi. "Solving #SAT and Bayesian inference with backtracking search". In: *Journal of Artificial Intelligence Research* 34.1 (2009), pp. 391–442.

[6] Velleda Baldoni, Nicole Berline, Jesus De Loera, Matthias Köppe, and Michèle Vergne. "How to integrate a polynomial over a simplex". In: *Mathematics of Computation* 80.273 (2011), pp. 297–325.

[7] Clark W. Barrett, Roberto Sebastiani, Sanjit A. Seshia, and Cesare Tinelli. "Satisfiability Modulo Theories". In: *Handbook of Satisfiability*. IOS Press, 2009. Chap. 26, pp. 825–885.

[8] Vaishak Belle, Guy Van den Broeck, and Andrea Passerini. "Component Caching in Hybrid Domains with Piecewise Polynomial Densities". In: *AAAI*. 2016. URL: http://web.cs.ucla.edu/~guyvdb/papers/BelleAAAI16.pdf.

[9] Vaishak Belle, Guy Van den Broeck, and Andrea Passerini. "Hashing-based approximate probabilistic inference in hybrid domains". In: *Proceedings of the 31st Conference on Uncertainty in Artificial Intelligence (UAI)*. 2015, pp. 141–150.

[10] Vaishak Belle, Andrea Passerini, and Guy Van den Broeck. "Probabilistic Inference in Hybrid Domains by Weighted Model Integration". In: *Proceedings of the Twenty-Fourth International Joint Conference on Artificial Intelligence, IJCAI 2015, Buenos Aires, Argentina, July 25-31, 2015*. 2015, pp. 2770–2776.

[11] Christopher M Bishop. *Pattern recognition and machine learning*. springer, 2006.

[12]   Andreas Bueff, Stefanie Speichert, and Vaishak Belle. "Tractable Querying and Learn-
       ing in Hybrid Domains via Sum-Product Networks". In: *KR Workshop on Hybrid Rea-
       soning and Learning*. 2018.

[13]   Roberto Cavada, Alessandro Cimatti, Anders Franzén, Krishnamani Kalyanasundaram,
       Marco Roveri, and RK Shyamasundar. "Computing Predicate Abstractions by Inte-
       grating BDDs and SMT Solvers". In: *FMCAD*. 2007.

[14]   Supratik Chakraborty, Daniel J Fremont, Kuldeep S Meel, Sanjit A Seshia, and Moshe
       Y Vardi. "Distribution-aware sampling and weighted model counting for SAT". In:
       Twenty-Eighth AAAI Conference on Artificial Intelligence. 2014.

[15]   Mark Chavira and Adnan Darwiche. "On probabilistic inference by weighted model
       counting". In: *Artificial Intelligence* 172.6-7 (2008), pp. 772–799.

[16]   Qi Cheng, Joshua Hill, and Daqing Wan. "Counting value sets: algorithm and com-
       plexity". In: *The Open Book Series* 1.1 (2013), pp. 235–248.

[17]   Arthur Choi and Adnan Darwiche. "Relax, compensate and then recover". In: *JSAI
       International Symposium on Artificial Intelligence*. Springer. 2010, pp. 167–180.

[18]   A Christofides, B Tanyi, S Christofides, D Whobrey, and N Christofides. "The optimal
       discretization of probability density functions". In: *Computational statistics & data
       analysis* 31.4 (1999), pp. 475–486.

[19]   Alessandro Cimatti, Alberto Griggio, Bastiaan Joost Schaafsma, and Roberto Sebas-
       tiani. "The mathsat5 smt solver". In: *International Conference on Tools and Algorithms
       for the Construction and Analysis of Systems*. Springer. 2013, pp. 93–107.

[20]   Alessandro Cimatti, Sergio Mover, and Stefano Tonetta. "SMT-based verification of
       hybrid systems". In: *Twenty-Sixth AAAI Conference on Artificial Intelligence*. 2012.

[21]   Barry R Cobb and Prakash P Shenoy. "Inference in hybrid Bayesian networks with
       mixtures of truncated exponentials". In: *International Journal of Approximate Reason-
       ing* 41.3 (2006), pp. 257–286.

[22]   Stephen A Cook. "The complexity of theorem-proving procedures". In: *Proceedings of
       the third annual ACM symposium on Theory of computing*. ACM. 1971, pp. 151–158.

[23]   Thomas H Cormen, Charles E Leiserson, Ronald L Rivest, and Clifford Stein. *Introduc-
       tion to algorithms*. MIT press, 2009.

[24]   Leonardo De Moura and Nikolaj Bjørner. "Z3: An efficient SMT solver". In: *Tools and
       Algorithms for the Construction and Analysis of Systems* (2008), pp. 337–340.

[25]   Rina Dechter and David Larkin. "Hybrid processing of beliefs and constraints". In:
       Proceedings of the Seventeenth conference on Uncertainty in artificial intelligence. 2001,
       pp. 112–119.

[26]   Rina Dechter and Robert Mateescu. "AND/OR search spaces for graphical models".
       In: *Artificial intelligence* 171.2-3 (2007), pp. 73–106.

[27]   James Dougherty, Ron Kohavi, and Mehran Sahami. "Supervised and unsupervised
       discretization of continuous features". In: *Machine Learning Proceedings 1995*. Elsevier,
       1995, pp. 194–202.

[28]   Hassan Eldib, Chao Wang, and Patrick Schaumont. "SMT-based verification of soft-
       ware countermeasures against side-channel attacks". In: *International Conference on*

Tools and Algorithms for the Construction and Analysis of Systems. Springer. 2014, pp. 62–77.

[29] Stefano Ermon, Carla Gomes, Ashish Sabharwal, and Bart Selman. "Taming the curse of dimensionality: Discrete integration by hashing and optimization". In: *International Conference on Machine Learning*. 2013, pp. 334–342.

[30] Evelyn Fix and Joseph L Hodges Jr. *Discriminatory analysis-nonparametric discrimination: consistency properties*. Tech. rep. California Univ Berkeley, 1951.

[31] Jerome H Friedman. "Multivariate adaptive regression splines". In: *The annals of statistics* (1991), pp. 1–67.

[32] Nir Friedman, Moises Goldszmidt, et al. "Discretizing continuous attributes while learning Bayesian networks". In: *ICML*. 1996, pp. 157–165.

[33] Michael R Garey and David S Johnson. *Computers and intractability*. Vol. 29. wh freeman New York, 2002.

[34] Marco Gario and Andrea Micheli. "PySMT: a solver-agnostic library for fast prototyping of SMT-based algorithms". In: *SMT Workshop 2015*. 2015.

[35] Timon Gehr, Sasa Misailovic, and Martin Vechev. "PSI: Exact symbolic inference for probabilistic programs". In: *International Conference on Computer Aided Verification*. Springer. 2016, pp. 62–83.

[36] Walter R Gilks. "Markov Chain Monte Carlo". In: *Encyclopedia of biostatistics* 4 (2005).

[37] Vibhav Gogate and Rina Dechter. "Approximate inference algorithms for hybrid bayesian networks with discrete constraints". In: *UAI*. 2005.

[38] Vibhav Gogate and Rina Dechter. "SampleSearch: Importance sampling in presence of determinism". In: *Artificial Intelligence* 175.2 (2011), pp. 694–729.

[39] Susanne Graf and Hassen Saïdi. "Construction of Abstract State Graphs with PVS". In: *CAV*. 1997. ISBN: 3-540-63166-6. URL: http://dl.acm.org/citation.cfm?id=647766.733618.

[40] Alexander G Gray and Andrew W Moore. "Nonparametric density estimation: Toward computational tractability". In: *Proceedings of the 2003 SIAM International Conference on Data Mining*. SIAM. 2003, pp. 203–211.

[41] Bernd Gutmann, Manfred Jaeger, and Luc De Raedt. "Extending ProbLog with continuous distributions". In: *International Conference on Inductive Logic Programming*. Springer. 2010, pp. 76–91.

[42] Dirk Husmeier, Richard Dybowski, and Stephen Roberts. *Probabilistic modeling in bioinformatics and medical informatics*. Springer Science & Business Media, 2006.

[43] Finn Verner Jensen, Kristian G Olesen, and Stig Kjaer Andersen. "An algebra of Bayesian belief universes for knowledge-based systems". In: *Networks* 20.5 (1990), pp. 637–659.

[44] Junmei Jing, Inge Koch, and Kanta Naito. "Polynomial histograms for multivariate density and mode estimation". In: *Scandinavian Journal of Statistics* 39.1 (2012), pp. 75–96.

[45] Michael I Jordan et al. "Graphical models". In: *Statistical Science* 19.1 (2004), pp. 140–155.

[46] Richard M Karp, Michael Luby, and Neal Madras. "Monte-Carlo approximation algorithms for enumeration problems". In: *Journal of algorithms* 10.3 (1989), pp. 429–448.

[47]   R Kindermann and JL Snell. "Markov random fields and their applications". In: *American Mathematical Society* (1980).

[48]   Doga Kisa, Guy Van den Broeck, Arthur Choi, and Adnan Darwiche. "Probabilistic Sentential Decision Diagrams." In: *KR*. 2014.

[49]   Samuel Kolb, Pedro Zuidberg Dos Martires, and Luc De Raedt. "How to Exploit Structure while Solving Weighted Model Integration Problems". In: *Proceedings of the Thirty-Fifth Conference on Uncertainty in Artificial Intelligence, UAI 2019, Tel Aviv, Israel, July 22-25, 2019*. 2019, p. 262.

[50]   Samuel Kolb, Martin Mladenov, Scott Sanner, Vaishak Belle, and Kristian Kersting. "Efficient Symbolic Integration for Probabilistic Inference". In: *Proceedings of the Twenty-Seventh International Joint Conference on Artificial Intelligence, IJCAI 2018, July 13-19, 2018, Stockholm, Sweden*. 2018, pp. 5031–5037.

[51]   Samuel Kolb, Paolo Morettin, Pedro Zuidberg Dos Martires, Francesco Sommavilla, Andrea Passerini, Roberto Sebastiani, and Luc De Raedt. "The pywmi framework and toolbox for probabilistic inference using weighted model integration". In: *https://www. ijcai. org/proceedings/2019/* (2019).

[52]   Samuel Kolb, Stefano Teso, Andrea Passerini, and Luc De Raedt. "Learning SMT (LRA) Constraints using SMT Solvers." In: *IJCAI*. 2018, pp. 2333–2340.

[53]   Daphne Koller and Nir Friedman. *Probabilistic graphical models: principles and techniques*. MIT press, 2009.

[54]   Daphne Koller, Nir Friedman, Sašo Džeroski, Charles Sutton, Andrew McCallum, Avi Pfeffer, Pieter Abbeel, Ming-Fai Wong, David Heckerman, Chris Meek, et al. *Introduction to statistical relational learning*. MIT press, 2007.

[55]   Alexander V Kozlov and Daphne Koller. "Nonuniform dynamic discretization in hybrid networks". In: *arXiv preprint arXiv:1302.1555* (2013).

[56]   Frank R Kschischang, Brendan J Frey, and H-A Loeliger. "Factor graphs and the sum-product algorithm". In: *IEEE Transactions on information theory* 47.2 (2001), pp. 498–519.

[57]   Shuvendu K. Lahiri, Robert Nieuwenhuis, and Albert Oliveras. "SMT Techniques for Fast Predicate Abstraction". In: *CAV*. 2006.

[58]   Helge Langseth, Thomas D Nielsen, Rafael Rumı, and Antonio Salmerón. "Mixtures of truncated basis functions". In: *International Journal of Approximate Reasoning* 53.2 (2012), pp. 212–227.

[59]   David Larkin and Rina Dechter. "Bayesian Inference in the Presence of Determinism." In: *AISTATS*. 2003.

[60]   Steffen L Lauritzen. "Propagation of probabilities, means, and variances in mixed graphical association models". In: *Journal of the American Statistical Association* 87.420 (1992), pp. 1098–1108.

[61]   Steffen L. Lauritzen and Frank Jensen. "Stable local computation with conditional Gaussian distributions". In: *Statistics and Computing* 11.2 (2001), pp. 191–203.

[62]   Steffen L Lauritzen and David J Spiegelhalter. "Local computations with probabilities on graphical structures and their application to expert systems". In: *Journal of the Royal Statistical Society: Series B (Methodological)* 50.2 (1988), pp. 157–194.

[63] Uri Lerner, Eran Segal, and Daphne Koller. "Exact inference in networks with discrete children of continuous parents". In: *arXiv preprint arXiv:1301.2289* (2013).

[64] Dangna Li, Kun Yang, and Wing Hung Wong. "Density estimation via discrepancy based adaptive sequential partition". In: *Advances in Neural Information Processing Systems*. 2016, pp. 1091–1099.

[65] Yi Li, Aws Albarghouthi, Zachary Kincaid, Arie Gurfinkel, and Marsha Chechik. "Symbolic optimization with SMT solvers". In: *ACM SIGPLAN Notices* 49.1 (2014), pp. 607–618.

[66] Yitao Liang, Jessa Bekker, and Guy Van den Broeck. "Learning the structure of probabilistic sentential decision diagrams". In: *Proceedings of the 33rd Conference on Uncertainty in Artificial Intelligence (UAI)*. 2017.

[67] Steven A Lippman and John J McCall. "The economics of uncertainty: Selected topics and probabilistic methods". In: *Handbook of mathematical economics* 1 (1981), pp. 211–284.

[68] Jesus De Loera, Brandon Dutra, Matthias Koeppe, Stanislav Moreinis, Gregory Pinto, and Jianqiu Wu. "Software for exact integration of polynomials over polyhedra". In: *ACM Communications in Computer Algebra* 45.3/4 (2012), pp. 169–172.

[69] Curtis Madsen, Fedor Shmarov, and Paolo Zuliani. "BioPSy: an SMT-based tool for guaranteed parameter set synthesis of biological models". In: *International Conference on Computational Methods in Systems Biology*. Springer. 2015, pp. 182–194.

[70] David Merrell, Aws Albarghouthi, and Loris D'Antoni. "Weighted Model Integration with Orthogonal Transformations". In: *Proceedings of the Twenty-Sixth International Joint Conference on Artificial Intelligence, IJCAI 2017, Melbourne, Australia, August 19-25, 2017*. 2017, pp. 4610–4616.

[71] Daniel W Meyer. "Density estimation with distribution element trees". In: *Statistics and Computing* 28.3 (2018), pp. 609–632.

[72] Alejandro Molina, Antonio Vergari, Nicola Di Mauro, Sriraam Natarajan, Floriana Esposito, and Kristian Kersting. "Mixed sum-product networks: A deep architecture for hybrid domains". In: *Thirty-second AAAI conference on artificial intelligence*. 2018.

[73] Stefano Monti and Gregory F Cooper. "Learning hybrid Bayesian networks from data". In: *Learning in graphical models*. Springer, 1998, pp. 521–540.

[74] Serafín Moral, Rafael Rumí, and Antonio Salmerón Cerdán. "Estimating mixtures of truncated exponentials from data". In: (2002).

[75] Serafín Moral, Rafael Rumí, and Antonio Salmerón. "Mixtures of truncated exponentials in hybrid Bayesian networks". In: *European Conference on Symbolic and Quantitative Approaches to Reasoning and Uncertainty*. Springer. 2001, pp. 156–167.

[76] Paolo Morettin, Samuel Kolb, Stefano Teso, and Andrea Passerini. "Learning Weighted Model Integration Distributions". In: *AAAI*. 2020.

[77] Paolo Morettin, Andrea Passerini, and Roberto Sebastiani. "Advanced SMT techniques for weighted model integration". In: *Artif. Intell.* 275 (2019), pp. 1–27.

[78] Paolo Morettin, Andrea Passerini, and Roberto Sebastiani. "Efficient Weighted Model Integration via SMT-Based Predicate Abstraction". In: *Proceedings of the Twenty-Sixth*

International Joint Conference on Artificial Intelligence, IJCAI 2017, Melbourne, Australia, August 19-25, 2017. 2017, pp. 720–728.

[79] Kevin Murphy. "A variational approximation for Bayesian networks with discrete and continuous latent variables". In: *arXiv preprint arXiv:1301.6724* (2013).

[80] Martin Neil, Manesh Tailor, and David Marquez. "Inference in hybrid Bayesian networks using dynamic discretization". In: *Statistics and Computing* 17.3 (2007), pp. 219–233.

[81] Davide Nitti, Irma Ravkic, Jesse Davis, and Luc De Raedt. "Learning the structure of dynamic hybrid relational models". In: *Proceedings of the Twenty-second European Conference on Artificial Intelligence.* IOS Press. 2016, pp. 1283–1290.

[82] Judea Pearl. *Probabilistic reasoning in intelligent systems: networks of plausible inference.* Elsevier, 2014.

[83] Benjamin Peherstorfer, Dirk Pflüge, and Hans-Joachim Bungartz. "Density estimation with adaptive sparse grids for large data sets". In: *Proceedings of the 2014 SIAM international conference on data mining.* SIAM. 2014, pp. 443–451.

[84] Hoifung Poon and Pedro Domingos. "Sum-product networks: A new deep architecture". In: *Computer Vision Workshops (ICCV Workshops), 2011 IEEE International Conference on.* IEEE. 2011, pp. 689–690.

[85] Luc De Raedt, Andrea Passerini, and Stefano Teso. "Learning Constraints from Examples". In: *Proceedings of the 32nd Conference on Artificial Intelligence (AAAI).* 2018. URL: `papers/aaai18_cl.pdf`.

[86] Parikshit Ram and Alexander G Gray. "Density estimation trees". In: *Proceedings of the 17th ACM SIGKDD international conference on Knowledge discovery and data mining.* ACM. 2011, pp. 627–635.

[87] Irma Ravkic, Jan Ramon, and Jesse Davis. "Learning relational dependency networks in hybrid domains". In: *Machine Learning* 100.2-3 (2015), pp. 217–254.

[88] Vanessa Romero, Rafael Rumí, and Antonio Salmerón. "Learning hybrid Bayesian networks using mixtures of truncated exponentials". In: *International Journal of Approximate Reasoning* 42.1-2 (2006), pp. 54–68.

[89] Stuart Russell, Daniel Dewey, and Max Tegmark. "Research priorities for robust and beneficial artificial intelligence". In: *Ai Magazine* 36.4 (2015), pp. 105–114.

[90] Tian Sang, Fahiem Bacchus, Paul Beame, Henry A. Kautz, and Toniann Pitassi. "Combining Component Caching and Clause Learning for Effective Model Counting". In: *SAT.* 2004. URL: `http://www.satisfiability.org/SAT04/programme/21.pdf`.

[91] Tian Sang, Paul Beame, and Henry A Kautz. "Performing Bayesian inference by weighted model counting". In: *AAAI.* Vol. 5. 2005, pp. 475–481.

[92] Tian Sang, Paul Beame, and Henry A Kautz. "Performing Bayesian inference by weighted model counting". In: *AAAI.* Vol. 5. 2005, pp. 475–481.

[93] Scott Sanner and Ehsan Abbasnejad. "Symbolic Variable Elimination for Discrete and Continuous Graphical Models." In: *AAAI.* 2012.

[94] Scott Sanner, Karina Valdivia Delgado, and Leliane Nunes de Barros. "Symbolic Dynamic Programming for Discrete and Continuous State MDPs". In: *UAI 2011, Proceed-*

ings of the Twenty-Seventh Conference on Uncertainty in Artificial Intelligence, Barcelona, Spain, July 14-17, 2011. 2011, pp. 643–652.

[95]   Roberto Sebastiani. "Lazy Satisfiability Modulo Theories". In: Journal on Satisfiability, Boolean Modeling and Computation, JSAT 3.3-4 (2007), pp. 141–224.

[96]   Prakash P Shenoy. "A re-definition of mixtures of polynomials for inference in hybrid Bayesian networks". In: European Conference on Symbolic and Quantitative Approaches to Reasoning and Uncertainty. Springer. 2011, pp. 98–109.

[97]   Prakash P Shenoy and Glenn Shafer. "Axioms for probability and belief-function proagation". In: Proceedings of the Fourth Annual Conference on Uncertainty in Artificial Intelligence. 1990, pp. 169–198.

[98]   Prakash P Shenoy and James C West. "Inference in hybrid Bayesian networks using mixtures of polynomials". In: International Journal of Approximate Reasoning 52.5 (2011), pp. 641–657.

[99]   Reid Simmons and Sven Koenig. "Probabilistic robot navigation in partially observable environments". In: IJCAI. Vol. 95. 1995, pp. 1080–1087.

[100] Russell Stewart and Stefano Ermon. "Label-free supervision of neural networks with physics and domain knowledge". In: Thirty-First AAAI Conference on Artificial Intelligence. 2017.

[101] Dustin Tran, Alp Kucukelbir, Adji B Dieng, Maja Rudolph, Dawen Liang, and David M Blei. "Edward: A library for probabilistic modeling, inference, and criticism". In: arXiv preprint arXiv:1610.09787 (2016).

[102] Dilin Wang, Zhe Zeng, and Qiang Liu. "Stein variational message passing for continuous graphical models". In: Proceedings of the International Conference of Machine Learning. 2018.

[103] Jue Wang and Pedro M Domingos. "Hybrid Markov Logic Networks." In: AAAI. Vol. 8. 2008, pp. 1106–1111.

[104] David Wingate, Andreas Stuhlmüller, and Noah Goodman. "Lightweight implementations of probabilistic programming languages via transformational compilation". In: Proceedings of the Fourteenth International Conference on Artificial Intelligence and Statistics. 2011, pp. 770–778.

[105] Frank Wood, Jan Willem Meent, and Vikash Mansinghka. "A new approach to probabilistic programming inference". In: Artificial Intelligence and Statistics. 2014, pp. 1024–1032.

[106] Jingyi Xu, Zilu Zhang, Tal Friedman, Yitao Liang, and Guy Van den Broeck. "A semantic loss function for deep learning with symbolic knowledge". In: arXiv preprint arXiv:1711.11157 (2017).

[107] Eunho Yang, Genevera Allen, Zhandong Liu, and Pradeep K Ravikumar. "Graphical models via generalized linear models". In: Advances in Neural Information Processing Systems. 2012, pp. 1358–1366.

[108] Eunho Yang, Yulia Baker, Pradeep Ravikumar, Genevera Allen, and Zhandong Liu. "Mixed graphical models via exponential families". In: Artificial Intelligence and Statistics. 2014, pp. 1042–1050.

[109]   Zhe Zeng and Guy Van den Broeck. "Efficient Search-Based Weighted Model Integration". In: *Proceedings of the Thirty-Fifth Conference on Uncertainty in Artificial Intelligence, UAI 2019, Tel Aviv, Israel, July 22-25, 2019*. 2019, p. 35.

[110]   Zhe Zeng, Fanqi Yan, Paolo Morettin, Antonio Vergari, and Guy Van den Broeck. "Hybrid Probabilistic Inference with Logical Constraints: Tractability and Message-Passing". In: (2019).

[111]   Pedro Miguel Zuidberg Dos Martires, Anton Dries, and Luc De Raedt. "Exact and Approximate Weighted Model Integration withProbability Density Functions Using Knowledge Compilation". In: *Proceedings of the 30th Conference on Artificial Intelligence*. AAAI Press. 2019.

[112]   Rodrigo de Salvo Braz, Ciaran O'Reilly, Vibhav Gogate, and Rina Dechter. "Probabilistic Inference Modulo Theories". In: *IJCAI*. 2016.

www.ingramcontent.com/pod-product-compliance
Ingram Content Group UK Ltd.
Pitfield, Milton Keynes, MK11 3LW, UK
UKHW050044180526
471099UK00006B/208